Get Off My Back

GET OFF MY BACK

Linda C. Maddox and Robert L. Maddox

Broadman Press
Nashville, Tennessee

Scripture quotations marked RSV are from the Revised Standard Version of the Bible, copyrighted 1946, 1952, © 1971, 1973.

Scripture quotations marked TLB are from *The Living Bible*. Copyright © Tyndale House Publishers, Wheaton, Illinois, 1971. Used by permission.

Scripture quotations marked GNB are from the *Good News Bible*, the Bible in Today's English Version. Old Testament: Copyright © American Bible Society 1976; New Testament: Copyright © American Bible Society 1966, 1971, 1976. Used by permission.

Library of Congress Cataloging-in-Publication Data

Maddox, Linda C., 1937-
   Get off my back.

   Summary: Explores pressures and problems faced by young people in such areas as family, romance, drugs, alcohol, fear, stress, and spiritual life. Includes case studies, suggestions for coping, and Scripture passages.
   1. Youth—United States—Social conditions—Juvenile literature.   2. Conduct of life—Juvenile literature.
3. Problem solving—Juvenile literature. [1. Conduct of life.   2. Adolescence. 3. Christian life]
I. Maddox, Robert L., 1937-   II. Title.
HQ796.M245   1987   305.2′35   86-21549

ISBN 0-8054-5344-X (pbk.)

To Andy, Ben, and Elizabeth

CONTENTS

INTRODUCTION

Have you ever felt that someone or something was on your back? Have you ever said, "I wish my mother (father, aunt, uncle, friend) would leave me alone—get off my back"? The language may have been different, but most of you have felt that pressure. Perhaps the back load is *something* rather than *someone*. In my years of experience as mother and counselor, I have not met anyone between the ages of thirteen and twenty who did not express similar feelings. In fact, I remember that busy day when the idea for this book was born.

I came racing to the telephone extension in the upstairs bedroom, in my usual way, and picked the receiver from the cradle to make a call. To my everlasting surprise and chagrin, I overheard Andy, our eldest son who was then about thirteen, on the downstairs extension. He blurted to his friend Dave on the other end of the line, "I wish my parents would get off my back!"

I was shocked! What could Andy mean? Had his dad and I been on his back? We did our best to guide him and honestly considered ourselves parents who talked with our children. In fact, we did all the "right" things: provided a comfortable and secure home, ego support, and involvement in our children's activities without meddling too much in their lives. Now, our son, in my eavesdropping ears moaned to his best friend that we, his very own, loving, concerned parents were on his back. That overheard conversation caused us to do a great deal of soul-searching.

Easing the phone down so he would not know I had mistakenly picked it up, I began a thinking process that has continued through the past decade. Conclusion: in the course of honest, earnest effort to do a good job as parents, we obviously, unavoidably land on your backs from time to time. Just as Bob and I have no inner need to stay on our children's backs, most of your parents have no need to stay on your backs. The dilemma comes in trying to find a balance between shaping, guiding, molding—even freeing— and staying "off the back." The goal of most parents is to enable you to become the best of which you are capable and to fulfill all that God intended for you.

After more than a decade of steady puzzling about teenagers, and after more than twenty-five years of working with them in school and church, we want to talk primarily with you about your problems and opportunities. We hope that parents will tune in also.

From these several years of keeping a sensitive ear peeled to teenagers, we readily admit that someone is nearly always on your back. Frequently the piggyback rider is a parent. However, just as often, the excess baggage is another teenager, a similarly important person, or a nagging problem, such as drugs, alcohol, stress, fear, death, or even religion. Whatever or whoever "it" is, we recognize it as a pain, a thorn in your flesh.

How to deal with "it?"

Survey the choices?

Grumble and grow?

Run away?

Deny its existence?

Or deal with the extra weight, honestly and creatively.

We are convinced that only by dealing with the problem will you regain and maintain control of your own back.

Again we repeat that we know all teenagers today have enormous pressures. All kinds of forces are on your back. Some you put there. Others just come from living in these topsy-turvy days. We would jump for joy if the book could point you in better direction so—

You could understand that you are not
    alone with your back load but that
    all your peers have something on their
    back also.
You could discover and use ways that others
    like you have handled similar situations.
You can successfully maneuver through
    these exciting but tricky waters of
    adolescence and young adulthood.

In the following pages you will meet teenagers and hear their stories. Some are individuals telling their story as it actually happened. On occasion, to protect privacy and not inflict fresh pain, we rearrange biographical facts while maintaining the heart of the individual story. Though a few of the stories take on a collective effect, all of them represent real-life situations we have seen and dealt with.

We know many of you could add a story or embellish those we have written. You may feel we have omitted your story. In some instances we did select extreme cases but we also left out many of the more bizarre, gruesome, spectacular episodes that, while adding a touch of spice, overstate the general condition of parent/child relationships.

Most of the time, we allow you to draw your own conclusions to the case studies. Occasionally we add specific teaching helps.

Since Bob and I are Christians to whom daily faith is quite important, we talk about spiritual dimensions and values. We find the Bible full of superb insights into the ways of people and God, so we will feel free to point you toward Scripture.

Frequently we will make use of materials and ideas from other books, teachers, and so forth. We enthusiastically insist a life is best lived and lived at its best when all the wonderful dimensions of human life function in harmony —mental, physical, familiar, spiritual, environmental, and political. We sincerely hope and pray you will come away from this reading adventure with measurably deeper insights into what makes you tick and a clearer view of how to keep ticking to greater purpose.

So, let's begin to get some of those unnecessary burdens off your back.

Linda C. Maddox

1
My Mother Made Me Do It

DOMINATION

"As I walked into the house, I heard my mother put the phone down. I waited—waited for all those inevitable questions and comments: 'Where have you been? Don't you know we were due at the Wilson's fifteen minutes ago? We've been waiting for you. Hurry and get dressed and do not wear that awful purple blouse. The next time you are gone I will see to it that that blouse disappears. I do not know where you get your taste in clothes—not from your sisters or me.'

"I had heard those same jabs so many times I knew exactly what to expect when I came home. The situation, the crisis changed, but the gripes would always have the same flavor. 'Why did you? Why didn't you? You must! You must not! Room not clean enough. Grades not good enough. Friends not quite up to standards. Boyfriend not right.' How can I live with my parents, especially my mother, on my back all the time?"

Shirley, the youngest of three daughters, lives in a small town. She is part of a strong, stable family. Without trying to make life difficult for Shirley, the two older sisters nearly always performed at the expected and accepted levels. By their nature, the older sisters did not create waves.

The girls' strong-willed parents lived intense, productive but rather predictable lives. Into this levelheaded, sensible family Shirley exploded as a fun-loving, academically underachieving teenager. Anything but slow in learning ability, Shirley had simply decided that grades were not going to be a "big deal" to her.

She could and did achieve success in other areas of life—cheerleader, life of the party, good athlete, true friend to all who crossed her path. But grades, discipline, and overall organization went sorely lacking. Her parents sensed, perhaps without really knowing for sure, that Shirley had made a decision not to fret over grades and discipline, hence much of the conflict between Shirley and her parents, especially her mother.

"My mother is extremely well organized—very businesslike. She's a leader in the church, the community, her clubs. I know she wants the very best for me, but honestly, she is *never* satisfied with anything I do."

The conflict came to a head and perhaps began to turn around over the issue of advanced biology. Even though Shirley's grades would not win her a prize, she did well enough to qualify for some of the accelerated classes in her high school. At the beginning of the school year, Shirley announced that she had decided not to take advanced biology. The work load was too demanding especially with cheerleading and all the other activities during the fall.

Her mother hit the ceiling. "What a poor choice, Shirley.

If you cannot do advanced biology and cheerleading, you can just drop cheerleading."

The battle was joined. Mother and daughter screamed at each other over the dinner table. In an attempt to restore some order and get on with the meal, Shirley's father interjected, "Shirley, as a compromise, please talk with your counselor tomorrow and see if she can talk some sense into you."

Shirley agreed. Anything to get her parents off her back.

The counselor suggested that Shirley take a few aptitude tests to see if any learning problems existed. Though the tests showed nothing new, they did provide a good handle for Shirley and the counselor. They revealed that Shirley had good ability, but because she had consistently been less than enthusiastic about grades and studying, she had missed enough information along the way to make it all the more difficult to make high marks. Adding to the problem of studying, Shirley's full-orbed social life made extra demands on her energy and time.

But What About Advanced Biology?

After several conversations with the counselor, Shirley and her mother agreed to a yearlong plan. Mother and daughter agreed to a contract of sorts. Shirley's mother would try, really hard, not to tell her every move to make. She would allow her daughter some room for disorganization and even some room for not studying, including not taking advanced biology. Shirley agreed to abide by the guidelines—curfew, use of the car, minimal room care, and so forth.

Shirley wanted freedom, freedom to fail even, with as little interference as possible from her mother. She also agreed to accept the consequences of her actions, such as repeating a course or a term if necessary.

Most important, the two agreed to communicate. Mother would try not to lecture. Shirley would listen and talk, reasonably, with her parents.

The first six-week grade period ended with Shirley's grades at the B and C level. No fuss from her parents. They expressed interest, but did not lecture. Shirley had chosen her own path and they would try to let her walk in it.

And the noise level in the household went down as conflict gradually lessened to "some" conversation. Her parents did not always agree with their daughter, yet they generally maintained the posture of discussion rather than negatives and threats.

A Problem

Near the end of the school year Shirley came bursting into the counselor's office. "I have a problem. A real problem." She burst into tears.

Shirley had just learned of an impending F in English. According to the teacher, Shirley had not turned in her poetry paper.

"But I did, I really did!"

The teacher had an extra poetry paper, but it had no name on it. Shirley could not prove it was hers. She did have a sheaf of scratch notes from which she had prepared the poetry assignment. The scrubby notes, even though they matched the unnamed poetry paper, were not sufficient to convince the English teacher that the unsigned document belonged to Shirley. (Actually Shirley and the teacher had feuded all year, neither willing to establish communication with the other.)

"What can I do? I do not want to fail."

"Call your mother!" the counselor declared.

"You must be kidding! She will only take the teacher's side. Mother always sides against me. And besides, she probably won't have time."

Shirley came bursting into her house and told her mother they needed to talk. The busy mother had an important meeting and was on her way out the door when Shirley had said, "I need to talk with you." The mother stopped, called the chairman of the meeting, asked to be excused, changed into more comfortable clothes, and sat down to talk with her daughter.

Shirley could not believe her eyes. Never before had she taken first place over anything in her mother's life, or so it seemed.

Next day Shirley and her mother had a conversation with the teacher. "I believe Shirley did the work. That unidentified paper you have belongs to my daughter. Please use the scratch notes and at least compare the work. I would like for you to give her credit for what she has done."

Disaster was averted.

In the course of this new arrangement, everything did not sail along smoothly. Shirley's grades did not go much beyond the B and C level. Most of the time her room kept its cyclone-just-hit-me look. What did happen, however, has more long-range promise. Shirley and her mother began the process of understanding each other, of accepting each other as people of worth and ability in spite of the ways they rubbed each other wrong. They established a new pattern of relationship that made life much more enjoyable in that household. Could it be that one dominating parent had just decided to get off the back of her teenager, freeing both of them to be not only mother and daughter but, best of all, friends?

Shirley's story may have worked out . . . .

BUT, . . . THERE'S ANGELA

Don't kid yourself. Some parents do try to live their lives over again in their children.

As far back as I can remember my parents showed me off. Fortunately, my father had the kind of income that allowed my mother to decorate the house and me.

From the earliest days that I could toddle around, they entered me in contests—baby, beauty, gymnastics, little miss whatever. I never remember liking any of the contests, but I never remember saying too much about it. Maybe I whined or complained, but I did not want to displease my parents.

It seems that I never could play and get dirty. I was like a doll designed for show.

My performing career started early. Every week my mother hustled me off to some kind of studio for training. I dreaded the recitals and shows, but always did well in them. My parents rarely criticized me after a performance. In fact, they nearly always told me I did better than anyone else. They just never let me stop. Speech, drama, piano— all came in due time to help me toward *their* goals.

As I grew older, the situation became even worse. I had to win any contest that I entered—beauty, dance, cheerleader, class officer. I had to win and I usually did because I worked so terribly hard.

On top of all those "things," I had to maintain top grades. I can remember practicing three of four hours then studying a couple more hours before falling into the bed, too tired to move—almost too tired to sleep.

My parents spared no expense to make me look good. I never feared doing poorly. I did fear not winning. I smiled and waved and no one ever knew what I felt during those performances. The applause did not do anything for me. Nothing made it worthwhile except the pleasure of my parents.

For a brief moment after high school, I asserted myself. I made the decision to go to college far away from my hometown. But I had no idea what to study. At the present, I still perform. I still compete in beauty contests. I am a cheerleader. But somehow I don't know me. I don't know what I want or who I am. I don't go home very much because I know that "they" do know what I should do. Without a doubt, there is a thread, though invisible, tied to every check they send me. They have so many hopes for me; plans that I don't want to know just yet. They have allowed me this space, giving me some time. Perhaps they are right, perhaps I will go home soon. They usually win. After all, without them I do not know who I am or what to do.

AND ANOTHER

Sam's father was just a regular guy with a good job. He went to work at 8:30 and came home at 4:30 with no other responsibility toward his occupation. That was perfect for him because his love was athletics. He worked with Sam until he found the best sport (or sports) for his son. His father spared nothing to help him develop his skills. To Sam's father, sports existed not be played but won. Athletics became the consuming passion of that household. Life was made for men and men were made to excel in some kind of sport involving a ball.

His father attended every practice and every game. Up and down the sideline, Sam's father moved with such fervor that bystanders often thought he belonged to the coaching staff.

After every athletic contest, Sam knew he would get a play-by-play account of his mistakes and only a brief word about any successes. Sometimes if he had done particularly poorly, Sam's father would make him sit alone in his room and think over the entire game, listing for himself all his mistakes.

Sam enjoyed athletics, but the pressure to do well dampened his feelings for the game and chipped away at his confidence. If Sam's father did not recognize it, Sam did. The young man, though a capable high school athlete, had only limited talent as a football player. Sam knew he would never win any scholarships or receive honors as an all-American. Nevertheless, he did what he could to satisfy himself and his father.

When asked why he knuckled under to his father's demands so meekly, Sam said, "My father is so strong, so determined. He wants only what is best for me. I have never bucked him in my life. I don't know that I could. Frankly, I have never had to do much thinking on my own. I am not sure I can make it without him telling me every move to make. Can you imagine what he would say if I told him that I do not "love" ball. Can you imagine what he would say if I told him that every season I hope that I break a bone so I will not have to try so hard just to make the team. Sooner or later I will tell him how I feel, but not right now."

SOMEDAY . . .

Sooner or later these teenagers who live so far apart, who are so different in cultures but so close in situations, will work to establish their own lives. It is true that adults can be so strong, so persuasive, so "right." And yet, you can be controlled and dominated only if *you* allow it to happen. No doubt you must wait, even wait to make your own decisions totally, but you can learn to stand up for your own thoughts and desires.

We can allow ourselves to be controlled by others in a score of ways. You can be controlled by doing everything to please others. Or you can be controlled by rebelling against everything to displease others.

The balance comes in learning to know yourself, to see your own gifts and talents as well as your own desires. What is in your best interest? Who are you? What gifts have you been given? The gift of life is also the gift to discover yourself. The easy way out is what Angela said, "I will probably go back. After all, my parents know what is best for me."

Maybe, maybe not. Coming to an agreement with your parents about your life would be great. But never looking at your self, your gifts, and discovering under God who and what you are is to miss much that life has to offer you. You do not want to live a life without some controls. The nature of life in society is to cooperate with laws, some traditions, and established codes of behavior. We make a mistake, however, if we let our lives become dominated by forces—people, habits, friends—outside ourselves. Set your own sails. Ask others to help you but accept responsibility for your own life.

TAKE A BREAK

Be not conformed to this world [nor anything in it]: but be ye transformed by the renewing of your mind, that you may prove what is that good, and acceptable, and perfect, will of God (Rom. 12:2).

Fathers [and mothers], provoke not your children to wrath: but bring them up in the nurture and admonition of the Lord (Eph. 6:4).

Honor your father and your mother, that your days may be long in the land which the Lord your God gives you (Ex. 20:12, RSV).

Come gather, children everywhere.
Come and listen. Come and see.
It is God alone who gives us our lives,
And God who sets us free.
Free to live. Free to decide.
To make our world what it will be.

And then it is God who demands that we die.
And that's just the way it is for you and me.

. . . .

If God is the One who gives us our lives,
Then children of God we must be.
But how can we be the children of someone we can't
    hold?
Of a Father we can't see?
And God can't be held. And God can't be seen.
But we meet Him whenever we're set free.
And we learn about freedom when we learn the way life
    is,
And that you and I decide how it will be.

> *And God likes me just the way I am.*
> *I turned out just right.*
> *But I'll sing it again in case I forget.*
> *And, strange as it seems, I might.* *

____

*Martin Bell, *The Way of the Wolf* (New York: The Seabury Press, 1968, 1969, 190), pp. 89-90.

2
More Than I Can Handle

DRUGS

Nothing made any sense to me. My eyes would not focus. My brain would not tell me where I was. People moved around in the room like ghosts; but I could not tell how many, who they were, and, frankly, none of that fuzziness bothered me in the least. I must have made some noises, maybe even asked some half-crazed questions because someone stopped, handed me a glass of water, a few pills, and something to smoke. I still do not know what they gave me, but in a few minutes I felt good again and drifted back to sleep.

I do not know how long I stumbled and slept around in that nasty, filthy house filled almost all the time with crummy-looking people, most of whom were complete strangers to me. Later I learned that my parents had begun to search for me soon after I dropped out of sight. They came to the city, asked questions, tried to trace my whereabouts, but could find no one who would help them. Finally, a close family friend located me. He called my parents and together they brought me home again.

It nearly blew me away when I understood later that I had lived in such a pigsty for several months. Talk about a lost weekend—I lost nearly six months!

As crazy as it sounds, when my family found me and started to take me home, I resisted. I could not make a decent decision because of my polluted brain.

I wish I could say that when I got home everything straightened out. Not so. You can always find the wrong friends. They have a way of just coming from the woodwork, from cracks in the pavement. I had hardly unpacked before I began to run into folks who could make me feel good by supplying me with drugs. Oddly enough, I did not have to pay for most of what they gave me. They were not really pushers, just kids who existed on drugs and always had some available.

Wonderful Me—In a Mess Like That?

How did I fall into that sorry state? It did not take long. It did take a few choices, a few turns in my life. I grew up in a Christian home. My parents always did everything to make life good for me. I never doubted their love, though I did not always understand or return that love. I never felt as grown-up or "with it" as everyone else seemed to in school. Though quite intelligent by all tests, I did have some difficulty learning. Attending a mixture of public and private schools, I made it through elementary school. About the time I completed elementary school, my parents learned of an outstanding school in a distant city. I did not want to go. My parents did not want to send me, but it seemed the best course if I were to develop adequate communication and coping skills.

I remember my utter panic when I saw Mom and Dad drive off and leave me hundreds of miles from home. But it turned out all right. I made friends and had a good time with other people. I had great fun flying home for the holidays with all the fuss and buzz of such trips. My family always made a big deal over me when I came home. Of course, I felt a little envious of my sister who lived at home all the time. It never failed, after a few days at home, I began to fight with my sister. I just chalked that up to the trauma of not being at home all the time.

After I graduated from school, I moved back home. That was mistake number one. I missed my school friends. My sister and I began fighting in earnest. I felt my own strangeness at home and so did she. We could not get along five minutes.

Frustration.

I wanted to be on my own. I wanted boyfriends. At school I had never lacked for dates. At home I hardly ever had a date. In my loneliness, I bumped into a group of friends who would take me in with no questions asked. I had a car and some money, and I could be funny. They liked me. They made me feel good in their groups.

Those new friends were into drugs a little. Not heavy stuff. Just stuff that made me feel good even when I was feeling bad. After a fight with my sister or parents, I would need a lift. My friends and their little chemical friends gave me the boost I wanted. For those few hours, I could forget my problems. To be sure, this was a new world for me. Up until that point, I had lived a sheltered existence with no intrusions to upset the normal flow of life.

Soon, only with these new friends and their chemical brand of excitement did I have any fun at all. When my parents caught on to what I did with those friends, we began to fight for sure.

After a while, I decided to move out. I decided to go to a new city and enroll in a school that had special training in a field I thought I might want to pursue.

I went through the motions of promising to leave drugs alone. Perhaps my parents had grown weary of our fight. Maybe they believed me or wanted to believe me. Finally, they agreed to let me go to school and to help me with money.

I enrolled in the new school. I did fine for the first few weeks but then loneliness mixed with the desire to have fun like I did with my friends back home crept up on me. As I said, it is not hard to find the wrong kind of crowd to run with. Right there in the school I found them.

Drugs, light at first, then heavy. Then along came those people who took me in. I told my parents I was moving and gave them a post office box number to send the money. Then I sort of disappeared and did not emerge until my parents' friend found me and took me home.

The constant use of drugs and the insane life-style had combined to completely mess up my mind. I could not put a straight thought together. The local psychiatrist recommended that we find an institution that specialized in dealing with kids messed up on drugs.

After considerable investigation, my parents settled on a schoollike institution in a distant city. Talk about a nightmare. You could not imagine what I went through. After the weeks at home with little or no drugs, I had my head fairly clear when I went into that place. That did not last long. I saw everything clearly, the people, the prison-like conditions they lived under, the torture-chamber atmosphere. The hospital administration kept the doors locked all the time. The patients fought each other. The nurses could not get along with one another. The doctors did not know what to do except give us medicine. And, believe me, drugs were readily available in that drug-rehabilitation hospital.

One afternoon during a rare outing alone, I decided to leave the hospital. Without bothering to notify the hospital or make any attempt to get my clothes and other belongings, I called a friend who lived in the city who, in turn, called my parents. They allowed me to come home. They had a ticket at the airport for me to use. "Come home." Wonderful words to me.

Home, Home at Last!

I must have looked awful when I stepped off the plane, for both my parents burst into tears and hugged me close. The next weeks provided the mental, spiritual, and physical space needed to turn me around. My parents and I talked more and better than we ever had.

Some disturbing questions bothered us:

Would I live at home, and if I did, could I get along with my sister?

What sort of friends would I pick up?

Could I, would I, leave drugs alone?

I honestly felt myself cured of the drugs. They had brought nothing but grief to me and everyone I loved. Sure enough, I have had no more trouble with the chemical world.

After a few months at home, nurtured by the love and faith of my family, I felt ready to venture to school again. I knew that I must learn job skills that would give me leverage in the marketplace, so here I am trying to face the future with confidence, without drugs. *So far, so good.*

NOT ME. NO REGRETS. I LIKE RUNNING AWAY!

Yes I am back home, but even now I am not glad. Running away was all that I expected it to be—freedom and fun. In fact, I came back only to avoid a run-in with the local police. My live-in boyfriend, who thought that I was eighteen and away from my family by permission, saw my picture on the milk carton and threatened to notify the police if I did not call my mother and tell her where I was. He panicked that he would be arrested for "taking advantage" of a minor.

What kind of life did I live as a runaway? Not bad! Of course, you will probably think that I don't demand much of life. Maybe not! Anyway, life at home was tedious. I have a straight but boring older sister. My mother works two jobs to help my stepfather with the bills. Both are fairly involved in their own lives but are never too busy to try to tell me what to do or what I am doing wrong.

After I went to high school, I discovered another world— an exciting one. My friends introduced me to drugs, harmless naturally.

I really do like drugs, and I know to be careful.

To be honest, school and family interferred with my social life. It was too much of a hassle to go to school. Besides

I never had enough time to do homework and party, too. The authorities at school stayed on the phone calling my mother and giving me lectures.

On an impulse, a girl friend and I decided we had put up with enough of this kind of bother, so we ran. We ran without anything except the clothes on our backs, except for some money we lifted from her mother's purse. Since we live in a Midwestern state, we decided that any direction would be good for us. Transportation had to be quick, cheap, and easy. We caught a cab to the nearest truck stop and hitched a ride. Easy as could be.

The drivers treated us great, entertaining us with the CBs and listening to our tales of woe. We jacked up our ages by a couple of years each. (I became sixteen. She became seventeen.) We decided to become sisters and to explain that our parents told us we could go. They not only gave us their permission according to our story, but they wanted us to go, a little tired of the responsibility. The truck drivers were generally sympathetic, giving us fatherly advice and even feeding us sometimes. None of the drivers tried to bother us. We were lucky at that point, I guess.

Since the first ride we got headed west, my friend and I decided to go to California, knowing that we would find other runaways there like us. It was a simple procedure to catch rides from one truck stop to the next.

Arriving in Los Angeles, we again felt excited. We immediately found a cheap motel for the first nights while we looked for jobs. This, too, was easy because we would do anything that came along so long as we could get some money. I got a job in a fast-food restaurant. My friend, who was interested in becoming a cocktail waitress, went to work in a fairly nice club. Her work brought her into contact with some men who offered us a place to stay. The tiny apartment was crowded, but no one seemed to mind. The guys were older and had their own lives. However, it was not long before we had our own lives, too. We found so many people like us—runaways, or people just out of jail trying to stay clear of trouble. And so generous, especially with drugs. We did not have to buy any drugs, yet we always had a steady supply. The money that we made went for a few clothes and food. Not a bad life.

Now, I did decide to avoid *some* of the drugs. It was scary to see the people who shot up. I did feel really bad about a young man who just sat around all the time. At some point in his life he probably had a good mind. I could tell that. But now, he just sat in the corner of the room. He's probably still sitting there.

For awhile I enjoyed sniffing cocaine, but I decided not to do that anymore. I saw too many young people all messed up on coke, and besides, it was too expensive. After awhile the only way a girl could feed a coke habit was prostitution and I did not want to go that way.

My friend and I decided to split up. We both met guys we wanted to live with so we went our separate ways, though we saw each other nearly every day.

Life just moved from one fun thing to another. We were part of a group, a big happy family. We could do whatever we wanted to do. Such fun. Such freedom. The best part was that I did not have to think, to worry about anything, especially school!

Then, my new world came to a screeching halt. After three months of this kind of living, my mother, still looking for me, had the police run my picture on milk cartons and on the television in the Los Angeles area.

Just my luck. Friends saw the picture and told me immediately. My age made them uneasy, especially my live-in boyfriend.

Of course, I know that if my mother had offered a reward, even a small one, I would have been turned in a dozen times. Money is always scarce in the group.

End of story. My mother sent me a plane ticket and said if I came home, the police would leave me alone. So I went home. No big deal. My friends were waiting for me when I got there. They couldn't wait to hear my story.

Of course, my girl friend, who came home when I did made up some stories about me and added extra details that never happened, but who cares? She was so involved with her boyfriend that she didn't have any room to talk about anything. My friends will believe me.

I can teach them some things about drugs. I really like drugs. I do not intend to stop.

About school, well, I don't know. They will make me go back, but I won't go much. I don't like school. I like drugs. I may run again. I have no regrets.

Epilogue: A year later, this young lady is a patient in a mental hospital.

CAN WE TALK A MINUTE?

The list of stories about drug abuse is long and involved. Hundreds of thousands of sharp young people fool around with drugs. Each of you could tell your own episode of teenagers who turn to drugs for companionship, as an escape from loneliness, as an avenue to adventure, or just because everyone else is doing it.

Taking chances with drugs does not make teenagers bad persons, but it certainly does expose you to terrible danger. Flirting with drugs can quickly push otherwise upstanding, dependable teenagers to a life of petty crime or wandering aimlessly in the shadows of normal life.

In writing this book we have exercised caution in making sweeping statements, but here we depart from that routine by saying: *If you have not taken drugs yet, don't. No if's, and's or but's.*

This chapter is not designed to teach you about drugs; though some more careful education would certainly not do you any harm. However, if you are a teenager who "wonders," if you have allowed "drugs to get on your back," or if you feel more involved with drugs than you want to admit, these next few pages can help you. Most of you are serious enough to pay attention to your own actions and to change your habits if necessary. We want to offer some suggestions to assist you in finding new directions.

First of all, give yourself a drug-abuse test something like this:

These days do you have difficulty with concentration, with faulty memory? Do you suffer increased feelings of paranoia and/or growing feelings of persecution?

Do you have intensified feelings of inferiority or depression, passivity (don't care) and loss of energy, more difficulty with close relationships, difficulty with speech, or increasing inability to express your thoughts in words?

Do you have greater impulses toward destructiveness, increasing feelings of aimlessness and hopelessness, a persistent conversation with yourself and others that drugs might really might be harmful?

If your answers to these questions are generally in the affirmative, you should persuade yourself to see if you have developed a dependency on drugs.

As a starter for a new direction, try this—go an entire month without drugs. That's right, go cold turkey for thirty days. (How do you feel right now when we suggest a thirty-day drug fast?) If you can manage the month, you will probably find you feel better without drugs and will want to continue the drug fast a while longer.

If you cannot last the month, you will have to face the unpleasant, even frightening fact that you have a fairly serious problem with drugs.

From the earliest days of your life you persistently asked the question *why?* of everyone and everything around you. That one-word question charted and marked your growth into the world about you. This is another time to ask that question. Why do you need to take a drug? Ask yourself, Why do I need drugs?

As corny as it might sound, looking at your own need for drugs is healthy. Take a few minutes and write down what you want or wanted from your life. Take a few more minutes and write what you want or wanted from drugs. How do the expectations mesh? Do they blend or clash?

As you poke around with that *why* question, you may realize you need to make changes in your life-style. Often in the midst of growth and change, teenagers seem to get swept along on a running tide even without their expressed desire. Don't hesitate to try to change conditions so you can again manage your life in a productive way. Get hold of your life and send yourself on a trajectory more of your own choosing. Open yourself to a faith in God that can anchor you.

You may need to find a new group of friends to run around with, as tough as that may sound to you right now. Your drug-oriented buddies may exert more pressure on you than you can bear.

If your dependency is severe enough, you may need to alter your environment, even to the point of changing schools. You and your parents will have to make that decision together. Remember, *no* price is too steep to get you back into control, to get drugs off your back.

In the search for help with a drug problem, you know, of course, no magic cure exists. In all likelihood you will need to call on the combined resources of several services to help you beat your problem. Your community has many professional people trained to help you. Talk with your school counselor, your minister, a social worker, a teacher or other adult in whom you have confidence. Look for a church youth group you can join. Group counseling can frequently help. Years of experience teaches us that rarely does a teenager beat the drug habit alone. You need some help. Everyone needs help at one time or another. Your time has come. Reach out. You will find someone nearby to help you. A word of caution: if the first person you reach out to cannot help you, do not give up. Look for someone else.

So far we have talked about an aggravating but not overwhelming drug problem. Let's be brutally honest for a moment. If you have a serious problem with drugs, become disoriented, struggle with deep psychoses, are hooked on hard narcotics, are strung out on speed, seriously depend on softer drugs, or feel completely out of touch—*yell*, yell really loud for someone to help you immediately! Call anyone you know, expert or not, and tell them the whole sordid mess. Get help! You are not alone. The people who really matter in your life will not reject you. They will nearly all eagerly reach out to help you.

However, and it is a positive however, most of you are not part of the really weird world of hard drugs. Most of you who are presently flirting with drugs are simply looking for adventure. Fooling with drugs may look fun and exciting. You can buy them easily and once couldn't hurt, you might be tempted to say.

Some experts think the social pressures and easy availability of drugs are so great, nothing will stop young people from experimenting with them. Perhaps. Perhaps not.

Remember, you have to make finally your own decision about drugs. No one can make that choice for you, no matter how much they might like to. If you have ventured or stumbled into the drug scene and decide not to decide anything decisive, you have made a decision.

How will you decide? Which way will you decide?

Personal maturity, more than age, becomes the key factor in decision making. Maturity shapes your attitude toward yourself and others. Maturity equips you to make a crucial decision (yes or no to drugs, for instance) and to live with the consequences of your choice. Maturity tunes you into other people and their healthy or unhealthy relationship to you. Maturity helps you ask: What does God want for me? You can claim His strength to keep saying no to drugs. You can claim His strength to say yes to a drug-free life.

Finally, you and I have to say up front that maybe you want so badly to join the drug crowd, you will run the risk of personal disaster. You surely do need to face the stark, frightening fact you *might* be one who experiments and ends up addicted, with your life a wreck. Some of the nicest teenagers we know have come to that sorry state in their beautiful young lives.

We have no neat and tidy finish to this chapter because the end is not yet written, for you or for anyone. Not us, but *you* write your own conclusion.

P.S. Whatever your decision today, remember you are not alone. Forces of family, the community, the church, the best of your friends, and your Heavenly Father walk with you.

TAKE A BREAK

My new life tells me to do right, but the old nature that is still inside me loves to sin. Oh, what a terrible predicament I'm in! Who can free me from my slavery to this deadly lower nature? (Rom. 7:24-25, TLB).

The Lord makes us strong! . . . Sing to Israel's God! (Ps. 81:1).

Dear Teenager,
God does not say to you today, "Be strong"—
He knows your strength is spent—
He knows how long the road has been—

How weary you've become, for
He who walked this earth along—
Each boggy lowland and each rugged hill,
    understands.
And so He simply says, "Be still,
Be still and know that I am God."
The hour is late and you must rest awhile—
Let life's reservoirs fill up, as slow rain fills
    an empty, unturned cup.
Hold up your cup, dear teenager, for God to fill,
He only asks that you be still.

—Author Unknown

1. Do I believe that through His strength I can make those choices that are best for me?
2. Pray now that He will help you to be still and know that His strength is yours.

3
It Seemed So Right

TEENAGE LOVE

Ted and I met the summer before my high-school sophomore year and his senior year when my family and I moved into a house across the street from his. His easygoing, kind, sweet personality, and good looks made him extremely attractive. We had hardly unpacked when I set my cap for him.

His parents were gone nearly all the time. His mother came home from her work, did a little housework, and fell into bed. She was worn out from the long day. Ted's father's work schedule changed almost daily so he was practically an absentee father. Basically, Ted and his younger brother took care of themselves. The lack of supervision did not seem to bother Ted but it took a terrific toll on his younger brother who finally had to have professional counseling to help him through some rough spots.

I couldn't call Ted religious, but he was straight as an arrow—no drinking or smoking, highly responsible. He and I became fast friends in a hurry. We began to date regularly but because of a basic shyness in Ted, we did not officially go steady until after more than three months. From the very first I appreciated Ted's ability to see the importance of right choices, but as time went along I grew unhappy with his unwillingness to make really tough choices easily. I also discovered that underneath the easygoing appearance smoldered an explosive, even cruel side of his nature that in time caused both of us a great deal of pain.

Almost immediately, going with Ted became a way of life for me. I did not show any interest in anyone else, boy or girl. As far as social life was concerned, his life became my life. I planned my schedule around his. I shared all his interests, almost totally laying aside any of my own. I had no social life apart from Ted. I became totally dependent on him. I told myself I was attracted to him so completely because I was more mature than other young people my own age, seeing life through different eyes. Later, when circumstances forced me to take some close looks at myself, I decided this consuming dependency stemmed from a feeling that I could not relate to my peers.

Mature or not, I was not like most sophomore girls. I did not giggle at frivolous events that tickled other girls. I could not stand all the silly fads they went through.

The lack of silliness, the serious way I approached life, which sometimes made me feel set apart and lonely, perhaps came from the fact that we had moved so many times during my early years. With another major move always lurking around the corner and a whole host of new adjustments, I guess I decided to take on a mature attitude so I could deal with the constant uprooting. But early in life I did discover I needed one friend, a boyfriend. As far back as I can remember, I always managed to have a special boyfriend who could help satisfy the social and emotional needs of my life.

Our first months together held nothing but immeasurable joy for both Ted and me. We did not have a ripple in our relationship. Looking back I see what a wall we built around ourselves, but we could not or would not see it then. When school started in the fall, our time together only intensified. Because of a quirk in the school district line, we attended different high schools. Our lunch hours coincided, though, and, with the open campus we had during noon, Ted could meet me and we could eat together. We never had to deal with anyone else even at lunchtime.

He loved football and played it with utter abandon all during high school. Playing with the team fulfilled many of his ego needs for athletics, contact with other boys, and participation in school activities. Even though he worked hard at football, he paid careful attention to me. He was always on time, bringing clever little gifts. He was the perfect gentleman in every way.

Love and Life Get Heavier

Our life together was perfect until football season ended. Then I began to notice a change in Ted. He became more introverted, critical of everything—including me. When we started dating I weighed 118 pounds. But with my inactivity and everything that happens to fifteen year-old girls, I gained nearly twenty pounds in less than six months. Ted began to shout "Go on a diet. Don't be fat. You look bad." There were other critical statements: "I don't like that preppy dress," And the worst for me, "You're too immature."

I loved him so much I put up with those awful cracks. I tried so hard to find out what made him happy. I tried to be what he wanted me to be. Even that was a problem because he could not say what he felt or what he wanted—just what he did not want. I think maybe he stayed confused because he did not have a male model to pattern. His father stayed gone most of the time.

Ted stopped giving me gifts. He grew careless in picking me up, in calling. I could see him just taking me for granted, growing tired of me, looking around for someone else.

Another important aspect of our relationship had come into the picture. When I turned sixteen, I persuaded my parents to agree for Ted and me to have sex. At first my parents nearly died. Premarital sex flew in the face of all their personal and religious beliefs. Finally they gave in, sending me to a doctor who gave me birth-control pills. My mother and father wanted me to know what I was doing. They were so afraid for me. I could think only about my love for Ted and how much he wanted to make love to me. I felt we had a love that would last forever.

Our lovemaking was exciting but serious for me. I regarded myself as much too mature to simply throw myself into bed with a boy. We had a rich, wholesome, mature sexual relationship—or so we told ourselves. We both felt responsible, quite grownup. We knew we were good for each other, and we certainly satisfied each other physically.

Even with the sex, however, as spring blossomed, our relationship began to die. I had hoped sex would provide the bond we needed. Not so.

Then came that black night when Ted said to me, "This is boring. I want to break up."

I became hysterical. I did not know what to do. We had gone on a date to a nearby city. When I went to pieces, Ted got real mad. He threatened to throw me out of the car at first, and then drove like a wild man toward home. I screamed and cried all the way home. He screeched up in front of my house and shouted for me to get out of the car.

"No," I yelled back. We drove for hours and hours. I cried myself nearly senseless. He had been telling me I was no good, now he was telling me he did not want to see me anymore.

As dawn began to break I stumbled into the house, fell into the arms of my parents and collapsed into hysteria again. It took me days to get myself together. Mother called a counselor friend who agreed to spend time with me. From that point on I began to pull myself together. The counselor became my friend as well as professional guide.

Getting It Together Again

I told Ted, "I'm turning my life around. In spite of all you have told me lately, I am not a bad person." He could see that I would no longer take his teasing and sarcasm. He decided, for then at least, he did not want to lose me. We went back together, but not steadily.

I lost twenty-one pounds in six weeks. I met someone at school I wanted to date and we went out for a few times. When Ted learned of my dates with the other boy, he came over to my house at 1:30 in the morning. He cried. I cried. We could not make our relationship work, yet we could not give each other up. I still loved him, but we both knew it was over, at least for now. We talked with my parents about the pain we both felt. All the talking took a lot out of me, but after months of this uncertainty and pain, I decided we had to break up.

I cannot dismiss the fact that we made love. We cared deeply for each other. We wanted to get married. Surely we had more than a physical relationship.

Through it all, we both learned so much. I realized that love is physical, emotional, *and* spiritual. During the excitement and passion of those days, I did not abandon my faith. I simply was not true to it. Though I unconsciously tried to put my faith in God on hold, my underlying religious commitment and training did not allow me to be comfortable with our sexual involvement. Ted did not have the religious commitments that I did which, in itself, would have caused us serious trouble down the line. The spiritual part of our relationship was missing, simply not there. That spiritual gap would have made a marriage all but unworkable.

Ted and I had one more session together. He came to my house, and we talked and talked. He wanted the chance to explain his feelings, to talk about his own growing understanding of his own needs. We both reluctantly admitted we were too young for all we had been through. We talked about the heavy sexual involvement that neither of us could adequately handle. For the first time, I admitted to Ted how guilty I frequently felt because of our sexual involvement. I knew what we were doing was far from God's best for us, yet I was so caught up in it all, I did not want to think about the Lord very much.

We talked all night long. When he did leave at daybreak,

we kissed, held each other close, and understood there would be no more.

A few times after that he tried to call me, but I did not want to talk with him. In time he began to date again which hurt me, really hurt. A moment of the old pain flared up—what will I do? I need Ted. I even moved to pick up the phone but pulled myself away and liked myself better for doing so. A few weeks later I sent back the gifts he had given me. That hurt. I cried.

Many months have passed, and I have met someone new. My need for a boyfriend has not gone away. I understand myself so much more clearly now, though, and have a better handle on keeping myself and the relationship under the right kind of control. He is a person with whom I can be real, a person with whom I can develop the kind of relationship we both know is best for us at seventeen years of age. We have talked about the past. He knows how serious Ted and I were. He and I share a strong Christian faith. That calls us to a higher level of living. We have decided to wait on the heavy sex until later, much later. We will make love after marriage, if we indeed get married.

Something brand-new has come in. I have always liked to sing. Lately I have sung in several of the well-known restaurants and shows in the area, something I enjoy doing. The compliments come freely and serve to further bolster my self-confidence as a person and as a performer.

Thanks to my faith, my parents, and the Christian counselor I still see on occasion, I have made great headway with myself. But don't let anyone tell you a meaningful relationship is easy—it can be terribly intense. I know. I could handle the love, for a while, but I could not handle the separation, especially after sex became so much a part of our relationship. Don't misunderstand me. Sex can be physically just as good at fifteen as at thirty. But I know that rejection at fifteen, compounded by sex, is harder to deal with.

So much of Ted and all he represented is past history. I have come a long way and have many more miles to go, but at least teenage love is no longer on my back.

KIDS GET LONELY, TOO

Teenagers and love go together like hamburgers and French fries, like pizza and a soft drink. Before you get out of high school, you will have a crush on someone of the opposite sex. Many of you will go steady with one or more people.

We don't want to upset you unduly, but we should warn you that such relationships seldom last forever. When the relationship comes apart, resist the temptation to jump off the bridge. You hurt really bad when he/she goes after someone else. With some effort and with the help of some friends, youth and/or adult, you can make it through the wrenching heartbreak.

Dating, going steady, are normal parts of adolescence. Here are clues about managing teenage love and caution flags about relationships that get too heavy too soon.

Among the many contributors to teenage love is loneliness. One of the major reasons teenage relationships get out of hand is loneliness that nudges you into unhealthy involvements.

Loneliness of itself is neither bad nor good. It is a basic human emotion. Every mortal who ever walked on the earth has felt alone at times. Loneliness, however, does play strange tricks on people, old or young. Loneliness can turn us in on ourselves, pushing us to build even a high wall of defensiveness around ourselves, making us woefully introverted. Loneliness can push us to a frantic social life, grabbing for friends, relationships, and activities to ease the gnawing pain of aloneness.

How we deal with the emotion it is important. The young people in the "Love" story reached out to each other to meet their normal, natural needs. No problem. They were lonely—she from moving so often and he from a lack of parental support.

They simply became too wrapped up in each other. Their affection for each other *narrowed* rather than *expanded* their worlds. Because of the intense relationship and the loosening of social attitudes toward premarital sex, they succumbed to natural sexual pressure on which the relationship crashed and broke apart.

Given the fact of universal loneliness and the need for love, let's look at some guidelines for teenage relationships that can keep love gone haywire off your back.

It is OK to admit loneliness.

It is OK to admit a need for love and seek fulfillment.

It is OK to get serious about a person of the opposite sex and be with them frequently.

Be careful about making the other person the sum total of your world. That's not wise at any age. No one, no other person, no matter how much you care for them, has enough life to become your whole world.

Every youth expert we know offers extreme caution at heavy sex during young years. The moral questions persist. But even beyond the moral questions, the emotional strains on you are severe. Your own sexual drives are high already. You are at the age when they are supposed to be intense. Heavy sex at your age can become consuming. Premature exposure to heavy sex frequently leads to promiscuity in adult life, making it terribly hard to form a lasting relationship in marriage. What's more, you will have extreme difficulty making good judgments in the midst of heavy sexual involvement. There is always the danger of unwanted pregnancy.

Ninety-nine percent of the time one or the other teenager gets hurt as a result of an intense teenage love affair. The hurt is intensified if heavy sex has been a factor in the relationship.

Let's talk about the management of loneliness and the need for love:

1. Tell yourself and believe it—you are a person of infinite worth. Really! Claim that self-worth.
2. Change your life to reflect that growing sense of self-worth. Make yourself attractive—lose weight, exercise, clean up your life. Pay the price to begin to be the kind of person you want to be. How to bring about the changes that reflect your new appreciation of self-worth?

How? By the power of love reach down inside of you and pull up the best of who you are.

By the power of what love?

Love for yourself. Yes, it is okay to love yourself.

Love of those who love you—parents, friends, relatives. No matter how lonely and unloved you feel at times, you do have people who love you.

And, most of all, love that God has for you. God loves you. He knows your name. In Jesus, He shows His love and gives us a way to love Him in return.

Draw on that great reservoir of love to help you get love of self, for others, and God in focus.

TAKE A BREAK

Some of God's Words About Loneliness

He [God] heals the broken-hearted and bandages their wounds (Ps. 147:3, GNB).

Do not be afraid—I [God] am with you! I am your God— let nothing terrify you! I will make you strong and help you; I will protect you and save you (Isa. 41:10, GNB).

You will not be left all alone. I [Jesus] will come back to you (John 14:18, GNB).

A Great Word From God On Love

Love is . . . kind, never jealous . . . never haughty or selfish. . . . If you love someone you will be loyal . . . no matter what the cost. You will always believe in him [or her], always expect the best, . . . always stand your ground defending him [her]. (1 Corinthians 13:4-5, 7, TLB).

Don't you know that your body is the temple of the Holy

Spirit, who lives in you and who was given to you by God? You do not belong to yourselves but to God; he bought you with a price. So use your bodies for God's glory (1 Cor. 6:19-20, GNB).

A Word About Human Love

To be deeply in love is, of course, a great liberating force, and the most common experience that frees. Ideally, both members of a couple in love free each other to new and different worlds. I was no exception to the general rule. The sheer fact of finding myself loved was unbelievable and changed my world, my feelings about life and myself. I was given confidence, strength, and almost a new character. The man I was to marry believed in me and what I could do, and consequently, I found I could do more than I realized.

—Author Unknown

Do you free the people you love?

Do the people you love free you and bring out the best of your qualities?

Tell someone today that you believe in him or her. In your own words tell that person about the love of God.

4
The Way Up and Out

POVERTY

In today's society many of us have a difficult time truly understanding the paralyzing effects of poverty and the underachievement that all too often accompanies severe economic hardship. We who have all the good food we can eat three times a day and more, cannot imagine a father feeling proud he can "put meat" on his family's table once a week.

ROBERT'S STORY

Robert lived in a situation like that. His father boasted of their eating meat once a week. Robert's family was a large, black family. It was a family with pride and determination to get ahead yet plagued by all the bad luck, ignorance, and misfortune that seems to attack those who are poorly prepared to compete in today's high-speed world.

The rural section of the country in which Robert grew up afforded little economic opportunity for disadvantaged youth except seasonal farm work. He could find employment in the grocery stores or fast-food shops in the nearby city, but how would he manage the twelve-mile commute from his house in the country? The family had one broken-down car that most often refused to run. Hitchhike? Perhaps. One of the first questions employers asked their youthful job applicants always snagged the Roberts of the world: "Do you have dependable transportation?"

Early in his teenage years, Robert found himself involved with the simple pleasure of smoking pot. The pleasure quickly lost its simplicity when the young man discovered he could not live without his joint. We have all read statements by learned drug experts that pot smoking is not addictive. "That's wrong," said Robert. "I can't go without pot for a day. I don't care what they do to me. I have to have some—every day."

His dilemma intensified. It was not, "How can I get a job so I can have some money?" It was, "How can I get some money so I can support my habit?" Imagine what his life of near abject poverty did to such a feeling of dependency. He had to find money to buy marijuana—his only pleasure in life.

Some of his friends, similarly caught in poverty and drug dependency, proposed a solution: Take what "really" belonged to you anyway. So Robert joined a group that made a practice of "breaking and entering."

In an odd way, Robert said, breaking and entering also became addictive though often not very beneficial financially. Often the gang hardly got enough money or goods from the crossroads service stations and grocery stores to buy a day's supply of drugs. Their small take certainly did not make the risk of imprisonment worthwhile. But they continued their petty larceny, ignoring the odds of capture and arrest.

Sure enough, before too many weeks went by, some of the boys, Robert included, were caught and drew sentences in the area's juvenile detention home.

Robert liked the center! That's right. His own home was crowded and cluttered. In spite of all the efforts his mother made to keep the place clean, it was too run-down and had too many bodies living in it to keep much order. The family did not lack for basic food, but the food was not good, especially compared with food in the center. Robert became a model inmate who loved the structure of having a bell wake him up, with a warm, clean shower down the hall and a hot breakfast in the mess hall.

What about the pot? Robert had no trouble making it through his days in the center, free from the drug. He attended the school classes, listened to counselors, learned his lessons, performed his assigned chores, and in every way functioned far better than he did on the outside.

While he was in the detention center, Robert and his counselors began to address a side of his nature the young man could only vaguely understand. For little or no apparent reason, Robert would fly into a wild rage. He would have no warning of the onslaught of a spasm of anger, and the circumstances that seemed to trigger the episodes varied. Perhaps if he had stayed at the center longer, he would have gained better control of that side of his life which erupted from time to time, causing him much grief.

When he had served his sentence, he returned to his poor, rural family home. Reentry proved tough. Fortunately, in the time frame of coming back, he and the high school counselor became friends.

Because of the angry streak in his nature, Robert had a

way of simply walking away from a difficult situation, even in the classroom. If something came along he could not handle, he got up and left the room. No word from the angry, frustrated teacher could stop him. Such unacceptable behavior landed him first in the principal's office and then in the counselor's office.

He described a fear about himself: with his rational mind he did not want to be a victim of poverty, drugs, ignorance—anything. His emotions, however, dictated pleasure, escape, freedom. Mixed in with these fuzzy feelings he admitted his addiction to breaking and entering. No longer simply the need for money to buy drugs drew him to crime, he thrilled to the sheer excitement of the act.

"At night, sometimes, I lie in my bed, all crowded in with two other brothers, and have to hold myself down to keep from getting up, sneaking out of the house, and robbing a store," he declared with intense passion in his voice.

One day the young man became so consumed with a desire to steal and to enjoy his drugs that he burst into the counselor's office shouting, "I cannot think straight any more. My mind won't work. What will happen to me? I will have to leave school!"

"Where will you go?" the counselor asked.

"I don't know. Maybe back to juvenile home."

"Robert, you no longer have that for an option. You have passed the age for juvenile detention. Prison, big time, is the next stop you you."

From former inmates he knew, Robert had heard the horror stories of prison life. He dropped his head and wrung his hands in despair.

Can you imagine the on-my-back feeling Robert had—

poverty, a pronounced measure of ignorance, an aggravating learning disability all mixed in with a psychological dependence on drugs and burglary?

Robert had one friend whom he admired, a young man who lived across the road. That young man had experienced the same "caught" feeling of poverty. However, the friend, rather than turning to drugs and other such artificial highs, had become a Christian and found strength in his church community.

The young man talked with Robert and attempted to get him to follow the same way. Robert tried, honestly tried, but without much success. In his crowded, generally chaotic home with his older brothers drinking, shouting loud profanity, and ragging Robert for his religion, the struggling pilgrim could find little to hang on to. He felt so crowded and pressured he could not think straight. He certainly did not like his addictions, but he could not seem to find what he needed in religion, even though faith had certainly made a big difference in his friend across the road.

As with so many of our stories, we offer no neat solution. The counselor and vocational rehabilitation staff arranged a job for Robert. They suggested he live in a dormitory so he could have more stability. But some of his brothers teased him about what would happen to him in the dormitory so he refused to live there. No doubt he would have preferred the dormitory, but at that stage of his life he could not deal with the negative pressures from his family. He stayed at home, managing to commute to the program center for work and some school activities.

At this writing, Robert still manages to hang on, perhaps

even make some progress toward wholeness and stability. The odds are formidable that Robert can make it.

To his credit, the young man reached out for help. He sensed the load on his back was much heavier than he could bear alone. Because he has consistently asked for help, Robert has never failed to find someone who would walk at least part of the way with him.

Robert has also kept up his friendship with the young Christian across the road. Perhaps Robert can someday find peace for himself.

UNDERSTANDING POVERTY

Robert's family's poverty, to use a fancy word, is *systemic* that is, their struggles with poverty have roots tangled deeply in the systems, the structures of the culture that surrounds them. No one could ever accuse Robert or his family of not working hard. They work at anything they can find to do, at any job they can physically travel to. Their employment and economic problems have origins in prolonged generations of ignorance, lack of dependable transportation, and the scarcity of jobs for which they were qualified.

What's more, systemic poverty does not easily yield to solutions. Americans have tried massive government programs with only limited success. Large industrial and agricultural interests, without even meaning to, slow the upward progress of families like Robert's.

Does that mean Robert will always be caught? Not at all. It does mean he will have a tough time getting poverty off his back. When a person caught in long-term poverty does reach out and pays the personal price to get out, certainly the best resources of the nation, in general, and of the church, in particular, should respond.

Those of us to whom such poverty is not a problem need to exercise extreme caution and sensitivity before we dump criticisms on the Roberts of the world.

MONEY STRESSES

You, too, may feel the stress of money. Your family may not live at the poverty level like Robert's, but money crunches can exert a powerful, crippling force.

For instance, look at the following examples of economic problems that weigh on teenagers' backs:

• The husband and wife both worked and made an adequate income. They provided the necessities for their children, but a gnawing insecurity in the father prompted him to put away most of what he made. He would not give his children any money and refused to help them go to college at all.

• The children were ages five and eight when their father left home. The mother works but simply cannot make enough money to make ends meet. Now that they are old enough to work part-time jobs, the children pool their money with Mom's, but lack of funds is a chronic problem.

• For generations the family lived near and worked for the steel mill. They all knew the industry faced tough times these days for a host of reasons over which they had no control. Some of their friends had managed to move to other parts of the country but home and family kept them rooted. Now the mill owners have announced its closing. The entire community faces devastation. Uncertainty, anger, and confusion stalk every family within miles.

WHAT TO DO?

Obviously we have no quick answers, but in most situations resourcefulness coupled with sacrifice can enable teenagers and their parents to work their way up and out.

At the risk of sounding insensitive, teenagers caught in such family crisis should do everything possible to complete as much education as possible. In our day education is the basic ticket up and out. The only way to find a good job when the time comes, is to have adequate education. Even if your community suffers from economic depression, many parts of the United States offer a bounty of jobs. The more education you have, the easier time you will have moving into the job market. Finish high school. Begin studying at a junior college or community college. Pay the price to learn a marketable skill.

Sure you will have some bad days, but work extra hard not to let the blues get to you. Every successful person you talk with will tell you about the tough time and the obstacles they overcame to make a go of their lives and careers.

People will help you, but you must help yourself, also. Robert and the other teenagers we talk about in this chapter have made it so far because they reached out for help. Try not to be discouraged when no one at first grasps your outstretched hand. Keep reaching while doing all you can and someone will respond—a teacher, an employer, a friend, a minister. You have a friend out there, but you must risk the reach.

RUN FOR YOUR LIFE

We have seen wave after wave of refugees flock to this country, fleeing war and terrorism in their own lands. These hundreds of thousands of displaced persons bring a new face to poverty.

Most of us have difficulty imagining that sometimes people must leave their homes and run away to find peace and freedom. Jennifer and her family enjoyed status, affluence, and a comfortable home in their native land. Jennifer remembers, "We had a nice house, a beautiful garden, servants, motorbikes, and all the other things we liked, plus we had friends and family."

Her father, an educated man, had served as an officer in their country's army. Military and civilian people alike promptly obeyed his commands without hesitation. Suddenly, without warning, the government changed and a new regime took over. Jennifer's father regarded himself as a professional soldier who would maintain loyalty to whatever government ran the country. He realized he was treading thin ice with the new authorities so he tried hard to do a good job and stay in favor with his superiors. Shortly, however, he knew he would not make it. He had two choices— resign and run the risk of being executed by the government or get out of the country the best way he could as quickly as possible.

Jennifer's parents wanted to shield the children from fear and uncertainty as long as possible, but the teenager understood the changes in her country and realized her father's altered status. She heard her folks whispering back and forth, caught their anxious looks, and sensed their deep anxiety.

One night her father told the children they would all be leaving the next day for a wedding in an adjoining country. "We had relatives in the other country. They really were having a wedding. I knew we would not be coming back to our beautiful home and wonderful friends. I did not question my father, but I did cry myself to sleep that night."

Next day the family packed lightly, taking only what one would for a brief trip. They walked out of the house as casually as possible, lest they arouse suspicion. Trying to mask their fear, Jennifer's parents boarded the airplane and left their homeland for good.

"For several months we stayed with our relatives in the neighboring country while my parents worked feverishly to secure permission for us to come to the United States. We had to be very careful for fear the secret police from our country would kidnap my father or murder him on the spot. We felt greatly relieved to receive visas to move to America.

"I remember the night we left for the United States. We took only the few items we had left home with. We all breathed so much easier when the plane took off. Our future was uncertain, but we were convinced we would find safety in the United States," she says.

"My father had managed to sneak some of our money out of the country so we were not completely without funds when we landed, but we certainly had only a small amount of money. We found a two-bedroom apartment in a crowded section of the city. My father had to work at a store—quite a comedown for a former military officer. He wanted to start his own business so he worked hard and saved every possible penny he could. Though he was well-educated for life in our country, he was not equipped to command a big job here. He could not take the time to return to college; besides, we had to go to school. We had never known what it was to be on the bottom side of society, but we learned. My brother and I went on 'free lunch' at school. We were glad for the food but felt embarrassed at the same time.

"I believe the changes have been hardest for my mother. The cultures are so different in our country compared to the United States. Since she stays home more than the rest of us, she has had a harder time learning English. And she simply does not cope well with our new lives.

"We have found opportunity in the United States. Nothing good comes without a price. My family and I are learning to adjust, to pay the necessary prices to make our way in America."

TAKE A BREAK

The Bible teaches us that God has great compassion on the poor. Through the Scripture's preachers and poets, the Lord communicates His concern about our economic well-being. Meditate on some of the following Scriptures. Maybe you could take a few minutes and jot down some thoughts that come to you as you read this chapter, especially if you and your family are experiencing financial difficulty. You can be really honest in your jottings. Ask the Lord why this has happened to you. It is OK to complain to the Lord, but also count the blessings you do have. Ask Him to help you not to wallow in self-pity.

Listen and then make some "your eyes only" notes:

The Lord is my shepherd; I shall not want (Ps. 23:1).

Seek ye first the kingdom of God, and his righteousness; and all these things [food, drink, clothing, etc.] shall be added unto you (Matt. 6:31-33).

But my God shall supply all your need according to his riches in glory by Christ Jesus (Phil. 4:19).

I can do all things through Christ which strengtheneth me (Phil. 4:13).

5
Too Much of a Good Thing

RELIGION

Religion on my back?

Impossible you say.

Not so. But even as I tell my story, I feel guilt. I feel as if I am betraying my own faith, my parents, maybe even my own life.

For a long time I have struggled with a terrible load of guilt placed on my back by well-meaning religious people. Their brand of religion might suit their needs, but it nearly destroyed me.

At five years of age I stood at the side of my mother's bed as she lay dying. No one told me that she was dying. I just knew it with the intuition of a child. All the grown-ups who stood around her bed kept saying: "What a saint of God she is. I don't know another person so good. She has been a witness to us all."

My mother had lain on that bed for all of my five years. I did not know her as a saint. I did not even know her as a kind and loving person. All she ever said to me was, "Don't make so much noise. Do you have to talk so loud?"

I wondered about her sometimes, but not very much. Anytime I came into her bedroom with her lying there, I always had a dark and uneasy feeling. So I did not go in her room any more than I had to.

Mother birthed me, but my older sister cared for me. Everywhere she went I toddled after her. No matter how much people tried to pick at me, pull at me, or get me to talk, I drew back, choosing rather to hang behind my sister's skirt. People called me shy. Some even called me "backward." No matter, I did not want to talk to most people, particularly those who came to my house during the weeks before Mother died.

I remember the day she died. Though I was only five years old, I can see, feel, touch, and smell the day like it was yesterday. A big crowd of people from the church pushed into the bedroom and stood there praying out loud, weeping, speaking in tongues, and raising their hands. And some, I remember, stood talking to each other about the weather, their ailments, or this year's crops, while life slowly seeped out of my mother. Finally her breathing got shorter and shorter, higher up in her chest and throat, and then she did not breathe any more. When she sighed her last, all kinds of noise and bedlam broke out as the people praised the Lord for her wonderful life. It bothered me so much I quietly slipped out of the room, went out on the porch, and played with my doll.

My mother had suffered from cancer for eight years—three years before I was born and all five of my years of life. Somewhere along the way she got involved in a religion that felt sick people needed to abandon all medical help and look only to God. Since I had only known her sick, I used to wonder if my birth somehow killed her. It took many years for me to get that notion out of my head.

Daddy died when I was thirteen. During those intervening ten years, he took me to church every day. That's right, every day. We probably did not miss going to church a dozen days in all those years. We attended our church, neighboring churches, revival meetings, healing crusades— all kinds of services. When sundown came, my only question was, "Where do we go to church tonight?"

In nearly all the churches the people "spoke in tongues" with someone else doing the "interpreting." I do not understand speaking in tongues, but the people made trancelike sounds. After they had finished their speech in an unknown tongue, another member stood up to give the interpretation so the whole congregation could understand what God had just told them through the unknown tongue. For the entire ten years the same message always came through from God: God was mad about something or other. He was not pleased with His people. If we did not repent and shape up, He would do all manner of bad things to us. If young people went to movies, if girls wore pants instead of skirts or cut our hair or put on jewelry, or if people took medicine for illnesses, God would pour out fierce judgment.

At every service the preacher had an "altar call." At that part of the service folks who needed to be saved were persuaded to come to the front of the church and kneel. Others who wanted to speak in tongues, were also urged to come forward. If a person from the congregation came forward, several others swarmed around, placing their hands on the person. They all prayed at one time, frequently in loud voices, sometimes in tongues, that the person would be saved, get the blessing, be healed, or whatever the person seemed to need.

As a child attending those endless church services, I lived with fear of the wrath and taboo of God. I would have no more worn a pair of pants, gone to a movie, or put on makeup than I would have flown to the moon. Never.

And yet there kept creeping up in my mind the question, "What's this all about?" A troubling question for a young girl reared in such a heavy religious environment. I never thought of rejecting God. But I did live with a plaguing notion that my father and his fellow believers were not on the right track, certainly that I did not want to be on the same track with them. And yet anytime the question came to the front of my mind I nearly choked to death from the oppressive feeling of guilt. How dare I question anything that took place in the house of God!

To make matters worse, my father suffered from epileptic seizures. As long as he stayed on his medicine, he had no trouble with the disease whatsoever. He could work, drive a car, take us places, provide a home for us. My father wanted so much to be a good Christian, to do the right thing. He would do fine until he would start attending a series of healing meetings. I always dreaded those meetings because I knew he would throw away his medicine. The preacher or some member of the congregation would say that if my daddy would trust God, throw away his medicine, and have faith, he would be healed. Almost without fail my father would throw away his medicine. Within a matter of hours, he would be in the grips of a terrible seizure. He frequently hurt himself when he fell. After a few days of that kind of terror, he would sheepishly get back on the medicine and immediately stop having trouble.

Time and again the pattern repeated itself. We went to one more healing meeting conducted by a particularly persuasive preacher. "Throw away those pills, inventions of the devil." Daddy did it. The next seizure, especially violent, killed him.

Why didn't he stay on his medicine? I did not blame God, but I did wonder why He would let people like that preacher run around talking folks into killing themselves. First they persuaded my mother to forego treatment for her cancer. Now they talked my father into throwing away his medicine. They both died. "Religion" killed both my parents.

Slow But Sure Progress

What have these years done to me? What has happened to me in the name of religion? At fifteen years of age I experienced a genuine religious breakthrough. A friend about my age invited me to attend church with her. The people in her church also spoke in tongues, but with a striking difference. The interpreter said God is happy. I could not believe my ears. Never in all my life had I ever heard that God could be happy, I thought He watched from heaven waiting for me to make a mistake.

Sometime during my sixteenth year I put on a pair of shorts, excited, but also partly expecting God to strike me dead. Can you imagine how I felt when a pain, a real cramp struck me in my stomach. That was God for sure coming to punish me for dressing so sinfully. I ran into my room and snatched those shorts off, convinced the devil had invaded my body. For a while I withdrew more and more into that "backward" person people said I was.

I have gone through periods of time when I did not attend church at all, simply unable to bear the burden of even walking into a building connected with religion. But those times of not attending left me feeling even more shriveled up inside. Along the way I decided I needed a church and Christians who genuinely cared for me, but I could not participate in a congregation that in any way resembled those of my childhood. With the guidance and help of new friends I have found a church that could speak to my religious needs without heaping guilt on me or making my skin crawl with horrible memories.

I have made progress in my spiritual growth, but sometimes I still have waves of guilt and terror about God and religion. Even though my friends and a few understanding Christians tell me God is not out to get me, I still have a hard time believing them. I guess I heard bad news about God for so long that it is difficult to hear good news about Him.

Today as a grown young woman I am finally finding out I am a person in my own right. I have found a church with a strong, positive assurance that God loves me for myself and that the mistakes I make can be forgiven. I cannot always forgive myself. I want to help others with this same problem. I am convinced God is on my side. Deeds done in God's name have become important to me, not because God will get me if I don't serve, but because I find peace and joy in serving other people.

What a shame we let superstitions and fears cloud our

loving, our faith, our thinking. Sometimes I still forget. Sometimes I am still afraid. Sometimes in the middle of the night I fall to my knees, pray for God's forgiveness, and get up still very much afraid. Those scars are deep. It will take time to get religion off my back and into my heart.

JUST ENOUGH TO MAKE HIM MISERABLE

"I guess I have just enough religion to make me miserable but not enough to do me any good," the young man blurted.

George had a reasonably good record for his first three years in high school. His family was stable. He had experienced no great difficulties with drugs, the law, and so forth, but the young man was just not happy. He bordered on depression.

Though not regular in church attendance, he and his family held membership in a local congregation and went from time to time. As a youngster, he had participated in some of the church's activities but lack of parental encouragement for such events and the onset of teen years had seen him drop out of all but occasional worship attendance.

Over a period of time, he and the pastor talked about his personal faith, his prayer life, his feelings about God. At first he gave the stock answers about being a Christian, even though he did not go to church very much. He certainly believed in God, and he prayed every day. He did not feel his prayers "got very far."

During one of those sessions, he opened the door to his mind. "When I pray and think about God, I do not get a good feeling. I feel God is out there somewhere. But He has little time for me. I feel guilty when I do not go to church or when I do things I know I shouldn't. I've gone to church enough to know God does not like the way I'm living. I just cannot seem to break through my bad feelings about God."

The young man resembles scores of teenagers we have known whose undeveloped religion poses more of a burden than a freedom. The fault, in the case of the young man, lies not with the Christian faith, but with his unwillingness and hesitation to push on in his religious beliefs and practices until he can find some relief. The Christian faith does put some moral limits on our daily living, but it also promises us a new way of life full of liberty, adventure, and a sense of purpose. God does want to tell our consciences not to do some things, but far more, He wants to point us a new life in Jesus, His son.

TAKE A BREAK

I know this: God is on my side (Ps. 56:9, GNB).

Those who trust in the Lord for help will find their strength renewed. They will rise on wings like eagles; they will run and not get weary; they will walk and not grow weak. (Isa. 40:31, GNB).

Therefore if any [person] be in Christ he [she] is a new creature: old things are passed away; behold, all things are become new (2 Cor. 5:17).

> I'm always running into walls and things.
> I fall down a hundred times each day.
> But I'll pick myself up,

Dust myself off.
I've decided that life is just that way.

And I create the world I live in.
By each and every choice I make today.
And when all is said and done
I'm the only one
Who can make the world
A better place to stay.*

*And God likes me just the way I am.
I turned out just right.
But I'll sing it again in case I forget.
And, strange as it seems, I might.* **

1. Is your religious experience one of positive living?
2. Do you believe that God is on your side and there to help you?
3. Do you carry a great deal of guilt around that hinders rather than helps you live a victorious life?
4. Take a few moments to count the ways in which you can make a positive impact on your world.
5. Thank God for His presence and help to you.

The Lord has appeared of old unto me saying, Yea, I have loved thee with an everlasting love: with lovingkindness have I drawn thee (Jer. 31:3).

---

*Ibid., p. 71.
**Ibid., p. 89.

6
Why Not Me?

DEATH

Death is on my back!
I wish I had died rather than my sister.
I should have died rather than my brother.
How can I live without my father?
Why not me? What right do I have to go on living when she is dead?

These are heavy thoughts, especially for young teenagers. When death strikes a family, all kinds of difficult even black thoughts creep in, afflicting everyone in the house including the teenager.

WHY NOT ME?

As far back as I can remember, I, the kid sister, was always the one in trouble. Whatever I looked at or did turned sour, got me in hot water, upset my parents, and/or caused a mess.

Maybe I felt that way because my older brother did everything right. He made good grades, sang solos in church from the time he could toddle around, played sports in a great way, brightened up any room he entered, had more friends than you can imagine, and always got invited to the parties. Special, that's the only way to describe Mark. And, what's more, he was very special to me.

As a little girl, I can remember feeling lonely or afraid upstairs when my parents made me go to bed early. Then I would hear Mark coming up the steps, and I wouldn't be afraid or lonely anymore. Just as he did everyone else, he made me laugh and feel good.

That night, that horrible Friday night, when Mark got killed will burn forever in my mind. It happened more than ten years ago, but I can still tell you exactly where I stood in our den when the police called to say Mark had been hurt. The memory of the fear, the sinking feeling, still haunts me like a ghost when I let myself think about it.

Mark and a friend had bicycled down to the park to play tennis. At sundown they got back on their bikes and ped-aled out of the park, heading home. Charlie led the way, with Mark bringing up the rear. Just as they got out on the road, a truck came roaring up behind them, swerved to the left, then cut sharply back to the right, and ran over Mark. I can hear the screams and feel the emptiness as if it were only yesterday. Little did I know that night was only the beginning of my nightmare.

Just about everyone in the town came to the funeral. The youth choir from the church sang "Morning Has Broken." We all cried and cried. My mother and dad could hardly walk they hurt so bad. My friends rallied around me. Everyone tried to talk with me and tell me they were sorry. But underneath it all, I wondered if anybody, anybody at all, was glad that I was still alive. Since I was the troublemaker, I wondered if it would not have been better if I had died.

After several days of awful pain, with people in and out of the house all the time, our lives began to settle into a routine, a terrible new routine without Mark's brightness and laughter.

Somebody said, "Now you will have to live for you and Mark." What did that mean? I thought and thought about what they said. Maybe I should try to live for both of us. I would surely give it a go.

I remember lying in my bed and promising God and Mark, wherever they were, that I would live for both of us. I decided to be good, to make better grades, to behave myself at school and church. I really meant it. But it did not work.

In school my friends and I talked all the time. The teacher constantly had to make us be quiet. Try as I might, I could not make myself want to study. Actually, studying had never been my best thing, anyway. I knew I could do the work, but I just did not want to. I never had, and now with Mark gone and our house so quiet, I was not about to sit still and pore over schoolbooks.

It was not just the death of Mark. It was the silence of despair, the fact that life would never be the same again. Whatever died with Mark, took the life out of our house. Laughter gave way to pain and drawn faces that said "death" every time I walked in. For weeks and months I dreaded to come home. Most of all, I dreaded those accusations that seemed to come from everywhere. "Why are you alive? Why do you still walk and talk? Who are you to laugh? Why are you not on that lonely hill underneath the dirt instead of Mark?"

I have to say that time has helped. Laughter and love have gradually moved back into my life. From a kid sister I have grown up in such a way that boys come around all the time. Grades and such are still not terribly important to me, but I get along. Yet, after all these years, I still have moments when I ask, "Why not me?"

MOTHER WON'T LET GO

Stephanie recalls: My eyes were closed. I felt asleep. But my mind refused to shut down. Samantha spoke to me: "Stephanie, understand Mother. Be careful with her. But tell her, tell her, please to let me go. Tell her to let me rest in peace. Her fight to bring me back is wearing me out. I am all right. Tell her to let me go!"

My eyes stabbed open. Had Sammie's visitation been a dream or had my dead sister actually spoken with me? My mind reeled. Is Sammie really OK? What happened? How can I live through these days? She could always talk with Mother better than I could. Why doesn't Samantha come to Mother like she did to me? Let Sammie tell Mother to let her go. How can I tell Mother to let Sammie go? Samantha's dead. Maybe I should be, too.

Samantha and I were sisters, though more like only children because of the ten years between us. All our relatives, and even Mother and Daddy, said that Samantha was always grown-up, even as a little girl.

Mother always had a lot of physical trouble—headaches, depression, and such. None of the doctors could explain why she suffered such excruciating headaches and depressions. My father took her to hospitals everywhere, but still she had those awful headaches. My mother always looked so beautiful and wore such gorgeous clothes, and friends had a hard time imagining how bad she could really feel sometimes.

Mother and Sammie acted more like sisters than mother and daughter. Lots of time I felt I had two mothers, two wonderful mothers. I loved Mother and Sammie so much. Sammie could always help mother through her rough times, probably more than anyone else. As I grew older, I began to notice that my mother leaned on my sister more than Sammie leaned on Mother. All the time, whether Mother felt good or bad, she and Sammie would sit and talk for hours and hours.

Sammie could stay in her room studying, writing letters, even poems sometimes, while listening to music. Not that she holed up there all the time. During high school she took an active part in our church youth group, sang in the choir, helped at camps. At school she worked hard, made outstanding grades, graduating first in her class. She got elected to all kinds of offices and played basketball.

What a contrast. I do not have a quiet bone in my body. I never did like to be alone for any length of time. Not that I did not enjoy myself, I just wanted to be outside, playing with friends, tramping through the woods behind our house, riding one of our horses. And noise is my best friend, especially loud music. I fretted about my grades but not enough to work harder to improve them. I did not do poorly but I certainly did not measure up to my sister.

I have to say our parents never did compare us out loud.

My mother and father let us both be ourselves. They did encourage me to study just to make better grades. I know that even if they did not say it out loud, they couldn't help but compare us. But they really tried to accept us both as we were.

Even though Mother and Sammie talked all the time, I honestly do not ever remember feeling left out of their conversations. I did not want to sit and talk. Life outside, with buddies, doing my own thing, appealed to me more than long talks about serious matters.

I loved Samantha and I loved my father and mother. I even enjoyed having two "mothers" and the extra attention I got until . . .

Immediately following her outstanding high school career, Samantha went off to a college about five hours from our hometown. To our surprise, Sammie became unhappy. This was the first time in her whole life that she ever was unhappy for more than a few minutes at a time. She made her usual good grades, but she did not enjoy life at the large university in the big city. Maybe one of the main reasons she did not have a good time came from the fact that she had fallen in love.

That's right. She had fallen in love with one of the high school heroes, a good looking, lots-of-fun-boy-from-a-good-family, football star, Kirk. He could be more fun than a barrel of monkeys. Unlike Samantha, Kirk cared almost nothing for school work. He encouraged Sammie in her studies, but he could not care less about going to college. He could do anything with his hands and soon landed a good job in one of the factories in our part of the state.

When both sets of parents realized how serious Kirk and

Samantha had become, they encouraged the young lovers to take it easy, date others, go slow. No way. No one could persuade those two young people they did not have an eternal love. (And, in a strange way, it became eternal.)

At the end of her first semester Samantha left the university, came home, and enrolled in a fine but smaller college within commuting distance from our house. Kirk worked at his job and dabbled with one or two courses in the junior college. They saw each other every single day that passed.

They had seen the movie in our hometown theater, so Kirk and Sammie announced they planned to drive to a nearby town, go to the movies there, and be back home before too late. Nothing unusual about that, it happened all the time, especially on weekends.

Coming home from the movie that Friday night on the road they had traveled hundreds of times, Kirk wrapped his nifty sports car around an oak tree. The sheriff said the young people never knew what hit them. By the time the man who glimpsed the accident in his rearview mirror could whip his car around in the road and speed back to them, Samantha and Kirk lay dead in the fallen leaves that crisp, cold November night.

Sometime after midnight the call came to our house that an accident had occurred. A police officer in a flat tone of voice "regretted to inform" my parents that Samantha and Kirk had "expired" in a car wreck. Would my father or the boy's father please come identify the bodies?

My father's groan and my mother's scream jerked me out of a deep sleep. Within a few minutes the pastor and other friends begin to arrive. Daddy and Kirk's father went to the hospital to do the grisly job of claiming the bodies. Mother simply stumbled through the house wringing her hands, hardly crying, mumbling all the while "Sammie's dead! Sammie's dead! It can't be!"

Like some kind of dark, somber dance, the next few days unfolded. People came from everywhere to tell us they were sorry. It was Thanksgiving season, but none of us gave much thanks. The parents, all four, agreed to have a double funeral and to bury Samantha and Kirk beside each other. Eternal love. See what I mean!

The night when Sammie died, death crawled on my back. How many times have I wished that I had died rather than her. Little did I know how helpless I would feel for years to come.

My father seemed to manage rather well. He cried a lot. But he had a business to run and did not have much time for long, drawn-out sadness. I could go outdoors, be with friends, take short trips, ride my horse, and attend school and church. And even though I missed Samantha something awful, I could survive. Except I did not know what to do with my mother.

"Oh Sammie, please come back and help mother. She's having those awful headaches again. Some days she can hardly get out of bed. I don't know what to do with her."

Did anyone ever say anything to me to make me feel guilty? No. But a death curtain rang down around everyone in my whole family. I know my thinking got twisted sometimes, but I felt that if someone in our family had to die, the best one to go would have been me. Sammie could help my parents through my death, but I could not help them through hers.

What can I do? For a long time now I have lived with

death on my back, like a shadow that forever comes and goes. I do not believe my sister wants me to carry her death around like I do. What's more, strange as it sounds, Samantha has been my comfort during these years, an unseen but definitely felt presence. Maybe if Mother would let her go, I could, too.

SOME CLUES

Some experts say the fear and anxiety about death is the central problem facing all human beings. This fear of death triggers the crazy, destructive things we do. In order to deny the reality of death, we drive too fast, live too carelessly, flirt with danger, trying, in a weird way, to prove we can beat death's stalk.

We all need to face the fact of death—our own, those of friends, relatives, or of an immediate family member. In most cases we have no way to prepare emotionally for the death of a loved one except for one who has lingered with a prolonged illness. Even then death comes crashing in as the unwelcome intruder. But, without being morbid, to have an occasional conversation with yourself and with others you trust about death can help you prepare for the inevitable. Death will strike you and those you love sooner or later.

Crystal cannot deny the death of Samantha any more than Melissa can deny the death of Mark. But neither can they forever hold themselves responsible nor labor under guilt because their brother or sister died. Crystal and Melissa had nothing at all to do with the deaths. Try as they might, the teenagers cannot make up to their parents the loss of a child. And really, neither of their parents want them to.

By telling their stories, by facing their guilt, Crystal and Melissa are looking death squarely in the face. No doubt, both of them tried to bury themselves in activities, maybe in rebellion against authority, and even said, "Why not me?" Still, they are dealing with the fact of death in a way that eventually can lead them to peace and wholeness.

Parents sometimes contribute to the bad feelings of their remaining children, without meaning to. Their grief can be so intense they can have unpredictable, even strange reactions to the death of a child. Not until one has been a parent can those feelings of love and loss be appreciated. In the aftermath of the death of a loved one, it is not unusual for children to have to help parents through grief, even as parents help children through grief.

Sometimes teenagers left alive after the death of a brother or sister get the feeling that their parents are angry at them for being alive. Pressures in the household will, no doubt, intensify. All we can say to teenagers living under that kind of stress right now is to try to understand the feelings of their stricken parents. Do not form lasting feelings toward parents during the weeks and months of fresh, painful grief. Experience shows that the passage of time gradually heals the worst of the hurt. The love and memory of the lost loved one will not go away, but the pain and agony will gradually be washed away by the gentle waves of time. Be patient with yourself and with other members of your family.

Teenagers who lose a brother or sister in death cannot live for the dead. These teenagers cannot do enough, live enough, accomplish enough to make up for the loss of their loved one, nor should they try. The best way to honor the dead, a parent, a brother or sister, a favorite relative or friend, is to make the most of our own lives, not for the dead but because we are alive.

TOO MUCH GRIEF

Several people in the parking lot saw him stumble. In the instant he fell, they thought he had simply tripped. But in the next second the bystanders realized he was terribly ill. Within minutes the emergency vehicle was tearing through the streets toward the nearest hospital.

"Dead on Arrival" the records stated. A massive brain hemorrhage had snuffed out his young life within seconds after it struck.

His attractive wife and children were absolutely devastated. It was so unexpected—right at the height of his career. They were so happy with each other. Gone, without warning.

Carolyn, his wife, tipped off into a pit of depression, retreating deeply into her own grief. The children, especially Jerry, her oldest son, a young teenager, tried to pick up the pieces of their lives, but as the months of their mother's grief bore down on them, the family began to unravel.

Jerry, assuming the role of the "man of the house" tried to pull his mother out of her grief. When he could not, the latent, unfounded, but real guilt he felt at his father's death, began to stalk him seriously. From time to time he tried to tell his mother of his deepest anxieties, but she could not hear him in her own grief-stricken condition.

If he could not help his mother, he would join his father.

In the still of the night, as he languished in his own deepening loneliness or in the cold sober light of day whose warmth had been lost, Jerry decided to take his own life.

After everyone had gone to bed one night, he slipped down to the den where his father had kept his pistol, placed the gun at his head, and pulled the trigger. Miracle of miracles, he shook so furiously as he pulled the trigger, the bullet missed its mark. It inflicted a serious but not mortal wound on Jerry and saved his life, and ultimately his mother's life in the process. Too bad it took the nearly fatal tragedy to shake her loose. She was able to get herself together again and begin to deal not only with her own grief, but that of her children as well.

THE TOUCH OF LOVE

Sometimes the heavy hand of death is softened by the touch of love.

About three years separated the two boys. In their younger years, though they both loved the outdoors, fishing, hunting, and so forth, the older son showed marked ability as a student, taking honors all the way through public school. The younger son simply did not pay the price for grades. He did love the high school band in which he played a trombone whose slide was almost as long as he was tall.

An engineering degree and Air Force pilot training awaited the eldest son, always with distinction.

"Whatever will become of Jimmy," the mother frequently moaned, speaking of the happy-go-lucky younger lad.

Teachers and counselors saw another side of Jimmy and recognized a bright mind stuck in "idle" for the time being.

They came back to the mother saying, "Jimmy will be just fine. You just wait and see."

Ripping a peaceful night apart, their father's first heart attack initiated a profound change in the quiet family. "From now on you mark time 'before and after' the attack," a friend counseled. True. From that frightening moment onward, family time had as its demarcation line, "The attack."

Wayne, their father, recovered quite well. With exercise and more careful attention to diet, he mended as strong as ever.

Among the changes wrought by the illness, teenage Jimmy began to shape up. Face to face with the mortality of his beloved father, something clicked in his bright young brain that said, "Time to get on with life." The time had passed when he could salvage much academic success from high school but college became a piece of cake.

On a shining, clear, summer's Saturday morning, Wayne felt that inscrutable pain in his chest, lay down on the cool green carpet in his living room to catch his breath, and died. With tears and tributes for years of service to church and community, Wayne was remembered and then placed in the gentle earth on Fain Cemetery Hill.

The two boys, one in his late teens and the other just into his twenties, their tough but gentle mother, and their ageless maternal grandmother who lived in the home, would carry right on. Steven drew his military career to a close and prepared to enter graduate school. Jimmy marched steadily toward his own college graduation with academic honors a sure thing.

Katherine, their mother, said one day, "I do not feel well. My stomach hurts. Better get it checked."

Within hours of the examination, the family doctor had them gathered around saying, "It is most likely cancer of a serious nature. We must operate immediately with some prolonged treatment almost a guaranteed inconvenience."

It just happens that way sometimes. When the surgeon did his work, he found widespread growth of a quiet, creeping lethal type of cancer. He did all he could but that was actually not very much.

"Boys," the doctor said, "your mother will need extensive and terribly uncomfortable treatment if she is to have any extension of life at all. I do not want to hold out a very rosy picture for you. She is quite ill."

What? Impossible! Their father had been gone less than two years. Now this!

When word got out in the church and community of the drastic nature of the illness, the question buzzed around, "Who will take care of Katherine?"

When her sons heard the question, with one voice they chorused, "Why we will, of course." And they did.

Steven shelved his plans for graduate school and moved home. Jimmy, only a few courses away from an early college graduation studied during the week, driving home on weekends to do his part and give Steven a break.

The treatment proved every bit as rough as the doctor had predicted. But her sons stayed right with her. Some days she was so weak she could not get out of bed. Only their hands could adequately care for their mother.

All her adult life Katherine had played the piano for

church services and civic clubs. She clung to an abiding wish that she could play the piano for church service one more time.

As is the course of such illnesses sometime, remission came—a breather, a measure of renewed energy. She and the boys went out to dinner for the first time in many months. And wonder of wonders, on Sunday morning she took her place at the piano and played for the congregational singing.

Within a matter of hours after the service concluded, the illness renewed its stranglehold on her frail body. By midweek the cancer unleashed even greater torrents of fury.

"Steven, Mother is in serious trouble," warned young Jimmy. One of the boys picked her up from the bed and held her in his arms while the other brother drove the all-too familiar route to the hospital. Their doctor, who had walked with them through such dark days, confirmed what they already knew—their mother had died on the way to the hospital, in the special care of her two sons.

"When you've seen someone you love suffer for days and months, you really do not want to call them back," they would say. They laid their mother beside her beloved husband, drove away from the cemetery with grief but also with an assurance that they had done all they could.

Carefully and methodically, with feelings mingled with a certain amount of studied stoicism, they closed down the family's affairs, and moved on to their own pursuits. Some age, much faith and love, and the guidance of faithful friends have combined to keep death off their backs. No doubt about it, there are times when those last months haunt their sleep. They understand that death is part of life but that it does not belong on their backs.

TAKE A BREAK

Human beings do not belong to one another. We are God's children. We belong to Him. It is by sheer grace that we are together for a time—for a little while.

We receive God's gift of another person in our lives with thanksgiving. But we must realize that this person is a gift. We cannot cling to or refuse to let go of one of God's children when He calls.

Jesus said to His disciples, "Ye now therefore have sorrow; but I will see you again, and your heart shall rejoice, and your joy no man taketh from you" (John 16:22).

Blessed are they that mourn: for they shall be comforted (Matt. 5:4).

I would not have you to be ignorant, brethren concerning them which are asleep, that ye sorrow not, even as others which have no hope. For if we believe that Jesus died and rose again, even so them also which sleep in Jesus will God bring with him (1 Thess. 4:13-14).

O death, where is thy sting? O grave, where is thy victory? Thanks be to God, which giveth us the victory through our Lord Jesus Christ (1 Cor. 15:55, 57).

Though I walk through the valley of the shadow of death, I will fear no evil, for thou art with me; thy rod and thy staff they comfort me (Ps. 23:4).

What is the greatest gift you have been given?

If you answered *life,* than take a few moments now to thank God for that gift.

The next time that someone experiences the loss of a loved one or friend, take the time to send a note or go by and express concern and understanding. Because of your strength, the gift of living can be enriched.

7
Amy's Story

PUBLIC LIFE

Governor of Georgia? At three years of age the fact that my father had just been elected governor of the state simply did not compute. I didn't know anything about the job and could not care less about the honor. I only knew one thing: we would have to leave Plains and move to Atlanta. I, for sure, did not want to move. And I let my parents know about my displeasure.

"What's wrong with Plains? Why can't Daddy be governor here? We've got our house. My grandmothers are here to look after me when Daddy has to travel. Besides, we have a telephone. Daddy can talk with almost anyone in the world over it—right here in Plains!"

I enjoyed life in Plains, Georgia, very much.

But move we did.

What do I remember about the new house in Atlanta? About my father being governor?

For one thing, I had to wear Sunday clothes a lot. Even then I did not like to put on stiff, new-smelling clothes. To this day I prefer my older, softer, "friendly" clothes, stuff I have worn for a long time even over the preppy clothes many of my friends like to wear.

Visitors who came to our new Atlanta house frequently asked the same questions: "How does it feel for your father to be governor?" "How do you like living in this big house?"

I quickly learned to say something profound like "fine" and go off and play.

After I got settled into the house in Atlanta, the governor's mansion, however, I really grew to like the place. My cousins came to see me there. At the time it seemed like the house had hundreds of nooks and crannies to disappear into when we played. The lawns and gardens around the house were beautiful, providing fantastic places to run, swing, ride bikes, hide, or just play with friends.

We joined a nearby Baptist church where I made lots of friends who came to my house and invited me to theirs. Pretty soon, I guess I liked the house in Atlanta almost as much as I did the house in Plains.

In those days the governor of Georgia could serve only one term. As Dad's term drew to a close, Mother told me we would be moving back to Plains. She gave me weeks of warning. But that did not help much. Leave my friends again! Just as I did not want to leave Plains, now I did not want to leave Atlanta.

But move we did.

I adjust well. Living in Plains again was not half bad. With grandmothers, cousins, and friends living nearby, I had lots of fun.

Soon after returning to Plains and getting unpacked, my parents began to travel all the time. In fact, they were gone nearly every day during the week, coming home only on weekends. They did call me every night to see how I was doing.

This time I understood more clearly, though not fully, my father's activities. He had decided to run for President of the United States. He and Mother and some of our friends traveled all over the country campaigning for office.

How did I feel about that?

I did not care about the campaigning. I did care about the election. I did not want him to win. If he won, we would have to move again, this time to Washington D.C. The politics meant almost nothing to me. I simply did not want to leave home and friends again.

I was ten years old. I cried and cried when I heard he had won the election. But we moved anyway—into the White House and the Washington scene.

But, like I say, I adjust well.

The move to Washington proved to be not so bad after all. I began to make new friends. As always, we joined a Baptist church, the one up the street from the White House, where I made a few friends. I made some good friends at school and could invite them home.

Many of my friends came from the families of some of the people who worked with my father at the White House. We were at the same functions and understood the different demands made on us.

The White House provides a great variety of things to do—television, first-run movies in the family theater, a swimming pool, a bowling alley, lots of games, and a beautiful yard. My father had a tree house built for me in a giant tree on the South Lawn.

I loved meeting the famous people who came and went. I

enjoyed the movie and entertainment stars, and athletes. Leaders of other countries, such as Anwar Sadat, spent time with us. The Pope came to see us, and I met him.

Mother made some arrangements about my having to dress up all the time and sit through long speeches. She let me attend pretty well what I wanted to and what was more appropriate for me. Mother allowed me to leave the event early or at an appropriate time.

My parents made an agreement with the press not to question me. Most of the time, the press people kept the bargain.

But the public was another matter. It seems like people in the country showed almost as much interest in what I did as in my parents' activities. Outside the White House people always asked me the same questions: "How does it feel for your father to be President? How does it feel to live in the White House."

Giving autographs was a pretty neat experience. When my father was governor, I would take my pad and pencil outside with me to "sign" for people. At the White House, unless the crowd was large, unruly, or time was short, giving autographs was fun.

In Georgia we had state troopers to drive us around but no Secret Service. That was an adjustment for my friends and me. Everywhere I went Secret Service agents accompanied me—to school, to friends' houses, to the zoo, shopping, no matter where. At times they bothered me, but I know how helpful they could be. If the crowd got too pushy or if it looked like someone might try to close in on my friends and me, the Secret Service would ease in and usher me away from the difficult or chancy situation. Even after moving back to Georgia I had complete protection until my sixteenth birthday. By that time, believe me, I craved the freedom to move around on my own. I made some good friends among the agents, but it was good to be free.

How was it being the President's daughter? Everyone wants to know.

I feel nothing but great pride for my father. I believe in him. I did not feel much more hindered from activities than any girl my age would have been. My parents never did say, "You cannot do 'this or that' because it might hurt your father." They did expect me to know right from wrong and to make good decisions, but that had nothing to do with my father's office.

With my parents, I traveled all over the world. And even though I was young at the time, I had a great time touring while my father and mother attended meetings.

My greatest hurt came when my father did not get re-elected as President. In their rush to help him, my family and close friends did not do much to warn me that he might lose. The news of the defeat hit me like a ton of bricks. I cried and cried. I hurt for him and all those who worked so hard to help him.

And I cried for me—we would have to move again.

I could hardly stand the pain of packing and moving back to Plains. It was terribly hard; it was the worst time ever. My life and friends were in Washington, D.C. No one could share those experiences with me except someone who had been there. I felt alone and somewhat cut off from the world as we moved back.

My time-tested ability to adjust once again came in handy, however. I decided to make the best of what was to me a difficult time. Sooner or later my parents would have returned to Plains to live, so moving back was less of a shock for them. Taking into account the pain of the defeat, they were actually happy to be back in that town so full of memories. And they both stayed as busy as they wanted to be, writing and making speeches.

But I wanted to leave.

Without taking anything away from Plains (that will always be home) or anyone who lives there, I wanted to leave. After a long time of talking and persuading, my parents agreed to let me transfer to a private boarding school when I became sixteen.

Who's on my back?

Like every young person anywhere, my parents are on my back. I have to rush to say they give me less of a hard time than do many other parents. But they do demand a lot of me; sometimes more than I want to give. Sometimes I feel pushed around. I suppose like most teenagers in the land I would say that they do not always understand me. And I certainly do not always understand them.

I have known some loneliness. Because of my father's positions in public life, I have been separated from some very good friends along the way.

Living in the public so much, I sometimes felt part of my parents' world. But still I felt far removed from their world, also. So much went on that I did not know about, or could not understand, that at times I felt cut off. Both my parents would frequently go extra lengths to include me, let me know what was happening, but still I felt far removed.

The public has extremely lofty expectations of highly visible people, including their children. For some I was never pretty enough; for others not plain enough; for some not fashionable enough; for others too religious; for others not religious enough; for others arrogant and smart-alecky.

Fortunately, and this is a great thanks to my parents and family, they never pushed me to be what others wanted me to be. If my parents demanded a lot out of me, it was for my sake and not to make me put on some kind of artificial public face. Quite to the contrary, they always insisted that I be myself, my best self, but me. They freed my brothers and me to develop our own faith, our own perspective on life. Such support and freedom have been a great help in dealing with the public that has, at times, been on my back.

I suppose for a long time to come I will have to struggle with the question, "What is it really like being the daughter of the President?"

There are certainly other children of other Presidents. Some may have had more trouble with the public or may have felt unusually pressured.

What will happen to me?

I don't know but at this stage I surely am going to make the best life possible, in spite of any loads on my back. Some loads will stay there. Some will go away.

My word of advice for other teenagers in the public eye— be yourself. Be your best self, but be yourself.

THE PRINCIPAL'S KID

Imagine the epitome of the high-school principal—tall, smart, dedicated to public service, especially education, deacon in the church—and you have a picture of Mr. Smithson. He had come from a small farm in the southern part of the state. Against all odds he finished high school, college, and graduate school. He resisted offers to teach in large city high schools, preferring to work in a county seat town much like his own hometown. In every way, he served with distinction.

Mr. and Mrs. Smithson had two children. The town never could quite figure out how such dependable, steady people as the Smithsons could give birth to two more care-free, happy-go-lucky children. They were the exact opposite of their parents. More so than their daughter, their young son listened to his own drummer. He could not care less about schoolwork. He lived to play.

With all their study in educational psychology, Mr. and Mrs. Smithson understood and appreciated their energetic youngsters. But many in the small town could not refrain from talking about the Smithson children, especially the son. Without meaning to, the public wanted to force the boy into their mold. And he resisted. Long before he could put into words what he felt about living in the public eye, Stewart determined to carve out his own life. He did.

Fortunately he avoided many of the worst pitfalls of youth, such as heavy drinking and reckless driving, but just about anything else was fair game—pranks, hooky from school, complete inattention to schoolwork, sloppy clothing, and disregard for social conventions.

Thoughtful work by their parents, coupled with some caring friends in the town and a pastor who helped them, got the children through the worst of their times. They gradually came to terms with the public of the small town that rested so heavily on their young backs.

You may not be the daughter or son of a governor or president, but many of you feel the pressure of having public lives. Perhaps your parent lives a highly visible life in your community, and you feel like everyone has some opinion about your behavior. It is an uncomfortable load on your back. Also, many of you have parents who are much more concerned about the public on your back. They make you feel that any false step will reflect on their standing in the community or hurt their reputation. "Don't embarrass the family name" is a common expression.

FEELING TRAPPED

Jim says, "My parents do not put nearly as much pressure on me as the people in the congregation of the church where he is pastor. The people love my dad, and, I suppose, think they have to protect him and his good name. Anyway, I often have to endure the whispers of well-meaning people, 'Now your father would not want you to do that. Be careful, remember that your father is the preacher. We'll have to talk with the pastor if you don't stop talking in church. We know that you don't want to do anything to hurt your father.'

Some of my friends join the pressure by adding, 'Don't you just hate being the son of a preacher? Guess you can't go with us Saturday night or you would get into trouble.' I do not hate being the son of a minister, but I do hate feeling trapped into having to think, feel, or do anything because of that. I want to make my decisions without feeling that somebody is watching my every move to be sure that I say and do and think the right things because my father happens to be pastor of the church."

Being trapped by the outside is bad, but I feel trapped on the inside. I feel trapped by the publicity that my mother gets. She is a well-known person, a celebrity. She belongs to everyone, very seldom to me. Her life is one big "busy," very organized. I can never spend any idle time with her. Whenever friends come over, they are impressed because she will spend a few minutes talking with them. However, they get as much of her time as I do—very much the same. When she is home for an afternoon, the telephone rings constantly or someone drops by to discuss business. All these things are very important! She is constantly distracted with her own life. The tragedy is that she would never understand my saying this; she is confident that I am well-loved, well-provided for, and so forth. After all, I smile at her public, say the right things to her public, and, generally, do well at hiding my true feelings. When I join her in public, there are the appropriate mother-teenager antics. But I truly hate all the publicity around our lives and I hate the public life that we have to live. I feel trapped.

How did Amy, the Smithson kids, and the others manage all that much public on their backs? More to the point, how can you manage your life if your family situation puts you in the public eye?

Be aware of what makes you tick. As you get older and gain a measure of independence, you will have to declare your own territory. We urge you not to do silly, dangerous things just to prove your own independence and self-identity. Do not hurt yourself while attempting to demonstrate your own personality.

Living in the public eye has some pluses if you can manage the negatives. You frequently get to meet interesting people. If your parents are in government, you gain invaluable insights into the way the country operates. You have some adventures that other young people might not have. Do not overlook the good while struggling with the difficult.

And, remember, you must finally accept responsibility for your own life. No matter how famous your parents may be, you have to make your own life. You cannot hide behind them or blame them when life gives you a rough shake. Perhaps they did not demonstrate the greatest measure of sensitivity to your hurts, but you waste your own time when you shift responsibility from you to them. You must live your own life.

TAKE A BREAK

If any of you lack wisdom, let him ask of God, that giveth to all men liberally, and upbraideth not; and it shall be given him (Jas. 1:5).

For thou art my rock and my fortress; therefore for thy name's sake lead me, and guide me (Ps. 31:3).

Trust in the Lord with all thine heart; and lean not unto thine understanding. In all thy ways acknowledge him, and he shall direct thy paths (Prov. 3:5-6).

You shall walk after the Lord your God, and fear him, and keep his commandments, and obey his voice, and you shall serve him, and cleave unto him (Deut. 13:4).

8
Why Did I Go Back?

ABUSE

"Why did I go back?" Janis moaned with racking sobs stabbing into her halting conversation while the social worker sat across the desk with a stricken look on her face.

Frances, the social worker, asked herself the same question, "Why did Janis go back?" Weeks and weeks of work, court orders, home visits, official complaints, a careful search for the right foster home all gurgled down the drain when Janis fled from the court-appointed foster family. Incredible, but Janis had gone back to that awful place where she lived with two sisters, one brother, a bedraggled mother, and a demonic, abusive father.

For many years teachers and friends were suspicious that Janis and other family members suffered abuse from the father. Their suspicions were confirmed the day Janis came to school spilling her story to the school officials.

"I cannot go home. I cannot live there anymore. I will not go home. No one can make me!" she wept. Janis's appearance underlined her tale of horror about her homelife. The teenager's hair was cut in gaps all over her head with no strand more than two inches long. The day before, her hair had hung down below her shoulders, beautiful dark brown thick curls.

Janis told her heart-breaking story:

"My whole family is crazy. I don't even want my name to be the same as theirs. My father is crazy and I hate him. His father is crazy and all his brothers. His sisters have horrible reputations. I do not want to be part of this family. They're all mean, everyone of them. My cousin, Joey, was chased out of the house by his daddy with a knife. My cousin, Lois, was held at gunpoint by her daddy. You probably think I'm crazy. Maybe I am, but I know I do not want to be like any of them! You may not even believe me; you may not think that such as this could happen in our town. You are wrong if you think that. In fact, I may be killed for telling you.

"As long as I can remember, my father beat all of us. He did not give any reason, and we hardly every asked. It did not matter what rule we broke or did not break, the belt was his quick and dirty answer. After I was about ten, the whippings slowed down, but the abuse and nastiness continued in many different ways. I could not leave the house. I did more chores than were necessary and he fussed at me anyway. I waited on Daddy hand and foot. I could always predict the results—yelling and telling me how horrible I was. Telling me that I was crazy, dumb, ugly, and unable to do anything right. When someone came around, he acted so loving, putting his arms around me, wanting me to snuggle, and pretend we were a loving family.

"These last few years have been especially bad because he is so afraid that I might 'go with a boy.' He accuses me of all sorts of bad things. He often compares me to one of his sisters who lives a very bad life.

"This last fight happened because I came home late. After pleading and pleading he let me get a part-time job. I enjoyed the job in spite of the fact that he accused me every night of slipping out with boys. Last night I was late getting home because I met a boyfriend, not someone I was dating, but a friend. I tried to explain to my father, but he would not let me. Instead he went wild, threw me down on the floor, sat on top of me, and chopped my hair like you see it. He shoved me around, yelling and screaming, then threw me into my room.

"Believe it or not, this is not the worst thing he has done to me, but it is the final straw. Once, when he got mad at me, I ran out of the house, hid in the bushes all night, and slipped back into my room early the next morning after he left for work. He's done so many bad things to us, I could not even begin to tell it all. It's too terrible to believe.

"Where is my mother in all this? She's so afraid of Daddy that she will not do anything to help us or herself. Most of the time she will deny that the incident happened, even with our bodies black and blue to prove that Daddy beat us up. She may hate him like we do, but she's afraid of 'losing him.' He has hit her, too. That's the worst part. My brother tried to protect her, just making my daddy madder and madder.

"You cannot imagine the mess at our house. And both of my parents would deny everything I say. Don't even bother to ask them. I tell you they are all crazy. I may be too, but I cannot go back to that house."

Janis went to the social-service worker who took her out of her home temporarily while the county authorities investigated. Under a temporary court order, Janis went to live with a family willing to help her. But Janis could not stay at the new home. Her mother called frequently, begging her to come home. The familiar home setting, though brutal and out of control, tugged at her. Her parents promised everything would be better if she came home. Of course, she wanted life to be different so much that she was willing to take the chance.

Janis went home. Nothing improved. She did not adjust. This time the abuse, noise, violence, and turmoil got to her. She could not cope. Thinking she could not leave again, she found her own escape: drugs and sex. She overdosed and woke up in the hospital. She ran away, but quickly let her parents find her.

Finally her mother mustered up enough courage to help Janis. She removed her from the local school and got her enrolled in one a few miles from home and new enough to maybe give Janis a fresh start.

The father, still a domineering figure, but somewhat more subdued because of the threat of legal action, allowed his family a bit more peace, for awhile. However, Janis admitted to feeling like a prisoner in her own home. The future does not look good for Janis. Why *did* she go back?

SURVIVING

Stan, a victim of abuse, decided to survive.

"We live in a pretty neighborhood. My father has a good job and provides for our financial needs. The terrible problem in my home comes because he is also an alcoholic. He starts drinking on his way home from work and keeps it up until he passes out at night. In the meantime, home is terrible.

"When I come home, I never quite know what to expect, except that it will be bad. Walking into my house is like walking into a pressure cooker. No one ever says kind words. My parents argue constantly. We sort of stumble from one loud crisis to another.

"We go to church. My parents take part in some community activities. Dad's friends know he will take a drink, but they do not realize what a severe problem he has.

"My problem is that I am expected to do everything at the house. I never have time to get all my schoolwork done because of the chores, but my parents expect me to make all A's. No matter how hard I try, and I try really hard, I never do anything right. My parents both complain at me. I get grounded at the drop of a hat. My homelife is such a miserable situation.

"Even though I make good grades and have some close friends, I feel like a failure. And I feel like such a fake! Everyone seems to think we have such a wonderful family.

"I feel so sorry for my mother. I want to stay and help her get out of the marriage, but I do not know how much longer I can take the pressure. I want to finish my high-school education so I can get away and maybe even help my mother, brother, and sister get away, but I just do not know if I can last much longer."

In desperation, Stan turned to a high-school teacher who, in turn, pointed him to the counselor and others who could help him cope.

To his high-school counselor Stan said, "I have to get

some help! I cannot think. I have times when I think I am going to blow my brains out. In fact, I have taken an overdose of pills, but I just slept off their effects. Please don't tell anyone this. I want some help but I do not want you to tell anyone. The family could not take the exposure. We are too visible in town. It would hurt my father's work, and I do not want that. In spite of the way he treats all of us, I love him and do not want him hurt."

Through participating in a group with other young people in similar home situations, Stan found the power to cope with his difficult life until he could finish high school. As shabbily as his father treated him, he learned at least to be grateful that he rarely hit him. By contrast, some others in the group had bruises and welts as testimonies to the degree of parental abuse.

Also through the group and under the guidance of some interested adults, he finally recognized that he could not change the situation but neither should he blame himself for all the tension. Stan could not keep his father from drinking and giving his family such a hard time. The teenager could set his own goals and, by depending on his own faith, chart short-term and long-term goals.

We all wish that abuse—physical, verbal, and emotional—did not occur. We wish that parents would not allow themselves to get twisted and frustrated to the extent that they take out their dark selves on wives (sometimes husbands) and children. The fact remains, however, that many teenagers literally have their parents on their backs, threatening to beat them into bloody pulps or reduce them to emotional basket cases.

What to Do?

All too often nothing happens except a repeating pattern of abused children becoming abusive parents. Fear, ignorance of available resources, and inertia take over the lives of the abused and they simply slog from one battered day to the next.

Don't fall into such a hopeless frame of mind if you live in an abusive home. People will help if you will reach out just a bit.

If your circumstances get beyond you, you can go to public officials, county or city children's offices, high-school counselors, ministers, and youth workers and ask them to advise you. Both public and private institutions offer foster homes, group homes, and other arrangements to help you escape from an intolerable home environment, if that is what you need.

In most cases, if the abuse is not life-threatening, it is probably better to try to stick it out at home until high-school graduation. If funds do not seem to be available for further education, you might want to think about the military. The various branches of military service offer an array of programs that enable a young person, male or female, to get further education, learn valuable skills, travel, and make new friends as a trade-off for some years on active duty. Experience teaches it is possible to work through the difficult home environment. Do not try to handle a tough home situation by yourself. Find a group. Find someone to talk with.

Above all, claim the fact that you are a person of worth. God and some friends love you.

MY MOTHER, THE ABUSER

My mother does not drink or take drugs, but, as hard as it is for me to admit it, she does abuse us. As long as I can remember, I have dreaded being with my mother. On one hand, I know she loves us and would fight to protect us. But, on the other hand, she literally fights us.

My mother, though college trained in a profession, does not work. She has chosen to devote herself to the care of my father, my sister, and me. Her parents live several hundred miles away so she seldom sees any of her family. My father's family likewise lives several states away. Mother does not like Dad's family at all, so we avoid trouble by staying away from them.

Our family does many thing together—church, vacations, outings, all of the school activities, and any other community events in which we participate. To our circle of acquaintances we are a "regular" family. I imagine that many people hate to see my mother coming, however, because she has such a sharp tongue which she uses constantly to complain that we, the children, my father, the family, never get a fair deal in anything.

Regardless of what the town and church might think, life at our house is rough. My mother gives us a hard time. She cannot cope with anything. From the time I started walking, I learned to get out of her way if I saw that "look" in her eye. It does not matter what happens, small or large, if she is in "that" mood, we know to watch out. In her rages she pulls our hair until it almost comes out by the roots. She will isolate us, lock us away in our rooms for hours without food or water. One time she got so angry she drove the car into the side of the house, doing a lot of damage to both. I could not describe her nagging and screaming. She gets positively incoherent and goes on for hours, making no sense at all. Any effort at explanation sends her into more of a rage. We seldom have a peaceful moment.

Between those frequent outbursts, she tells us how much she loves us and needs us. Then she will go on about how nervous she feels, how many worries she has. She tells us how frustrated she becomes when we don't do what she wants.

The next verse of her song tells us how fortunate we are to have parents who love us, who provide for us, and who give us a good home, plenty of food, and warm clothes.

My sister and I have always tried to do as she asks, but her demands are impossible. Anything can trigger her episodes. We cannot bear the emotional and physical abuse she dishes out. As we get older, the slaps and licks with any handy object really get to us. I can see the day coming when I will no longer put up with her abuse. I will at least leave, if I do not hit her back.

Dad stays away from home, working all the time. I used to feel sorry for him because of the long hours on the job and also for the way Mother talks to him when he comes home. I do not feel sorry for him anymore. He could stop her abuse, to us and to himself, if he wanted to.

I also used to think he did not know what happened to us when he was on the job. If my mother beat us up and left marks, she would explain that we fell, or that she spanked us and we welted up like that. He pretended to believe her. He never took up for us. Now I realize that he lived a lie as much as she did.

What can I do?

I will not tell the authorities. But I had to tell someone. I had to have someone to give me some encouragement or some help. I am nearly through with high school and will go on to college. Sometimes I get so tired of listening to the mess from my mother that I cannot think. Sometimes I act like a jerk to my friends and teachers though they have nothing to do with my problem. They know only vaguely that my mother can act strange. Why do I treat my friends in such a rotten way? What can I do to get through these next years?

THE UNMENTIONABLE

No one in this whole world knows what I am about to tell you, and I mean no one. Maybe there's no reason to tell now because all that is in the past. But I want to tell you. Maybe someone can help me figure how it is going to affect my future.

From the time I was nine until I turned fourteen, my stepfather had sex with me. I never said one word to anyone about what he did to me. I did not know what to say or how to say it. Neither my mother or any of our friends had any clue at all that he ever did anything out of the way to me. He always conducted himself just right in public. My stepfather and mother worked different schedules so frequently they were not at home with me at the same time. I dreaded to see her leave for work because I knew he would probably come into my bedroom.

At first I was too scared and humiliated to do anything

but lie there. As I got older, I felt he had ruined me. I felt nothing but terror that I could never have a decent relationship with a man.

When I was fourteen, just a year ago, I started rebelling about everything—schoolwork, housework, curfew. I had a terrible feeling of being caught, trapped, unable to make any sense of my life at all. My mother simply could not understand what had made me change so much.

Finally, in a moment of rage and gross impudence, after my stepfather had again taken advantage of me, I blurted out, "Well, you must like me a whole lot better than Mom."

He looked like I had slapped him. I had never said a word about his sexual abuse before. He did not say anything, but from that day on he never touched me again.

Even though he stopped coming to my bedroom, I could not pull out of my anger and depression. I kept the whole house in a stir so, in desperation, Mother sent me to live with my father and his wife.

You would not say that my dad and I have a close relationship but we do have a good relationship. He does not know how to share my deepest feelings but he has never failed to reach out to me when I asked him.

After a few months with him, I have begun to get my life together. My grades have picked up. I keep the hours he and I agree on. He certainly feels good because he has helped me through my rebellious period.

He does not know what I went through with my stepfather, nor will he ever find out from me. My father would go after my stepfather and cause a huge scene if he knew. It would destroy my mother if she found out. No, I have decided that none of the family needs to know what happened to me during those earlier years.

Will I ever lead a normal life? Will I always feel so guilty about what happened?

These questions and more remain unanswered for Phyllis though she is working through the prolonged agony inflicted by her stepfather.

The stable environment of her father's home will help. By making better grades, enjoying the steady, if somewhat distant, affirmation of her father, she can begin to feel good towards herself.

Did she make the correct decision in not telling any of her family about the sexual abuse? *No!*

We say this without any hesitation: Do not feel "obligated" to take sexual abuse. *Tell someone! Protest!* Even though Phyllis took the abuse for a long time she finally had had enough and reacted to end the incest. She sought out someone to talk with—her counselor, and told her about her past.

Stories of other young people, similarly wounded, show that productive lives can be lived in spite of sexual abuse. Young women who have experienced this kind of abuse will have to stay particularly sensitive to their own feelings. Some form of ongoing counseling may well prove necessary—a professional, a school counselor, a pastor, someone who can provide guidance through the maze of confused feelings.

We know young people who have made wholesome lives for themselves, who have married, and had families. Unfortunately, we have known others who did not make it.

Important keys to success:

• Try to find a place of reasonable stability, if nowhere else, within your own being.

• Talk to some trusted person about the experience.

• Through faith in God and a growing self-acceptance, overcome guilt and personal dislike.

As in all these abuse situations, hate for parents or others who inflicted the pain, proves self-destructive. Forgiveness toward those who did the hurting will come, even if slowly. But you must work at forgiving. In the long run, carrying around loads of hate on your back can hurt *you* as much as the actual violence you suffered.

TAKE A BREAK

And they that know thy name will put their trust in thee: for thou, Lord, has not forsaken them that seek thee (Ps. 9:10).

When my father and my mother forsake me, then the Lord will take me up (Ps. 27:10).

He shall call upon me, and I will answer him: I will be with him in trouble; I will deliver him, and honour him (Ps. 91:15).

Be strong and of a good courage, fear not, nor be afraid of them: for the Lord thy God, he it is that doth go with thee; he will not fail thee, nor forsake thee (Deut. 31:6).

For ye are all children of God by faith in Christ Jesus (Gal. 3:26).

Behold, what manner of love the Father hath bestowed upon us, that we should be called the sons of God (1 John 3:1).

Have you ever felt that you could not win no matter how hard you tried?

A tiny pearl is formed by the pain and suffering of an oyster. No one expects a person to like to suffer or hurt. But as you work to change your situation, can you also work to become a stronger person inside?

Pray: "Lord, something has to happen. Do something, anything. Change our lives. This is no way to live. Lord, take over."

Write down three dreams you want to see happen to you in your lifetime. Start praying about those dreams and keep trusting God to help you.

9
Tales of Broken Hearts

DIVORCE

"What do you mean my parents' divorce has nothing to do with me! If their divorce is strictly between the two of them, why do I hurt so much? Don't tell me this divorce is none of my business," Julie sobbed to the support group.

All the young people in the group understood what she meant. Each had lived through the breakup of their homes. They knew the utter helplessness she felt.

As Julie wept and wrung her hands, members of the group unconsciously pulled in closer to her, lending their struggling friend their best emotional support. The unspoken warmth and concern of the group had a quietening effect on Julie. When she got hold of herself, she continued with her story even though her frustration and raw anger still came through.

"I don't remember when I first learned my parents did not enjoy being with each other. I am an only child and as far as I can tell, I have been the glue that held the family together. You name it and I have tried it to keep my parents

115

together. I have played them off against each other. I have planned little fun family outings.

"The first serious breakup came when I was around six. My mother, a beautiful lady, decided that she had to have some space, that she wanted some freedom from my father.

"Oddly enough, my father did not put up a loud fuss when Mother announced her intentions to move out. That's the way it always was at our house. My folks could decide to separate, have affairs with someone else, have strong disagreements, but they never raised their voices at each other. The weirdest decisions were made with hardly a cross word.

"My parents regarded themselves a 'beautiful, broadminded' people. If one needed a new wrinkle in the marriage, the other tried to accept it without too much complaining. After all, they both had successful careers, received invitations to all the 'right' parties. Of course, they would be civil and decent about their open marriage.

"But decent or not, the lack of love between them and the regular separations nearly destroyed me.

"When my mother decided to take her space, she took me with her. Even though money was in its usual short supply because of my parents' constant overspending, Mother got a small but nice apartment in the same town where we had lived together. That way my friends, the few that I had, and my school did not change.

"Let me give you a tough scene for a young girl who loved both her father and mother: I sat on a stool in the living room of the apartment, quietly pretending to play with my doll, while my mother and her new boyfriend got acquainted. She never knew how angry I became at her.

"I do not want you to think the whole problem lay with my mother. No one could call my father an angel. He had his freedom and flings, just like my mother. Through the years he moved out his share of times. After a cooling-off period, they would get back together. I would be so happy and my parents would look happy with each other—at least for awhile.

"I learned quickly how to manipulate my parents back together again. I would call my father or mother, depending on who I was not living with, and tell him or her how much I loved them, how lonely I felt, how much I wished they would get back together.

"This pattern repeated itself until I was in high school.

"I grew up much too fast and with far more information about life than I needed or cared to know. I could never pretend to be the naive girl my friends were. However, I could pretend about my parents, and I played an innocent game with my friends when my address would change.

"As a young teenager, I rebelled at everything. Sometimes I simply wanted to get back at my parents, cause them pain like they did me. Looking back on some of the silly things I did, I know now that I frequently felt so lonely and frustrated that I made a pill of myself just to get their attention.

"Fortunately I grew into a reasonably attractive teenager. And, in spite of all the turmoil at home, I managed to make fairly good grades. I enjoyed lots of popularity in high school and never lacked for a date as I got older.

"None of my good qualities mattered a bit, however, to my parents when their various split-ups came along. While bragging on me about my good grades, they could calmly pack and move out. As I got older, I would stay with my mother until we clashed, then I would go across town and move in with my father—that is, until they got back together as they always did until this time.

"I cannot patch up this separation. They will divorce. I don't have any doubts. Both parents have other partners—my mother a younger man and my father a longtime friend. I will never have a family again. I do not have any brothers and sisters. Mother and Dad are all I have. It is not fair."

As the others in the group listened to Julie, they could identify with her since their own pain was so fresh. Each, however, had a different reaction to what she said. As they talked with Julie about her situation, they also found measures of new strength and healing for themselves.

FOUR MOTHERS

For instance, John, a handsome teenager who looked like he had the world by the tail, tried to cover up his hurt as had done since he was two years old. "Don't take it too hard," he said. "Divorce is not so bad. It has not bothered me much. My father left my real mother almost before I could remember. In fact, we have had three mothers at our house since then. I certainly do not recommend my way to anyone else, but you can adjust. I have learned to let the women come and go. My sister and I just do not get involved with my father's wives and girl friends.

"I love my Dad. We know he loves us. He never misses our school events. My sister and I know his first commitments are to us. He just has lousy judgment when it comes to women. They look great. They simply do not last very long with my father.

"My mother lives in a distant city. She has had several husbands since she left my dad. My father has always made a good living so he and my mother agreed long ago we would stay with him. Once or twice a year I go see her for a few days. She and her husband or boyfriend always treat me great. I have a good time, but I never even consider staying with her.

"My sister and I have learned to stay the same. We keep our own habits. If we want to clean up our rooms, we do. If we want to eat at home, we do. If we want to watch television until late into the night, we do. His "wives" understand this is our home. The "mother" is the new kid on the block. She can fit in or move out. We do not argue or talk back to her. We are not disrespectful, but we don't necessarily do what she says if that means changing our basic lifestyle.

"At some point in my early high school years, I *decided* I would make good grades. So I have. With a reasonable amount of study I can stay in the upper 10 percent of my class. I also decided I would work hard at sports and have enjoyed some good recognitions as an athlete, especially football. My good academics and athletics make my father feel good and he never fails to give me a good word. I gave up long ago telling my real mother about my achievements. She hardly seemed to notice when I told her. So, I said, 'What the heck!'

"About the good grades and participation in school activities, let me explain. Other friends have gone through similar family situations with their parents; separation, divorce, hassling back and forth. So often, my friends let all this turmoil get to them. They don't study. They become wallflowers. They run with the wrong crowd and get in trouble.

"I decided the only way to make something of my own life perhaps avoid some of the heartache I have known was for me to make something of my life. If I did not take care of me, no one else would, that's for sure. Good grades, a good outlook on life in spite of all the upsets in my home are my tickets to a better life.

"Along the way I decided to become a doctor. My high-school science teachers have worked closely with me, helping me get a solid foundation before I go to college. They've been great. I have every intention of going to college, playing sports either in a club or maybe for the school's teams, and studying hard. I will be a doctor, someday.

"I have some good friends, an understanding minister and his family, concerned teachers, and to a good degree, my father and the Lord to thank for where I am."

With a warm smile, John turned to Julie and said, "Look, you can make it through this hurt. I know."

Then he gave Julie and the rest of the support group another word of advice coming from his "wisdom" as a high-school senior: "All of us might as well make the best of our situations. We cannot change anything about our parents. I try not to think too much about what might have been. Just take advantage of what you have and go with it. I know most of you pretty well. You have lots of abilities. Make the most of what you have. If you mess up, you will finally have only yourselves to blame."

THERE IS LIFE AFTER DIVORCE

With that word from John, Ginger piped up. "John, you and Julie don't know how bad I've got it. All you have ever known is family upset. Imagine my surprise when my parents announced that my father intended to move out for a few weeks while he and my mother thought about their relationship. Of course, they said that none of us children should worry about this new arrangement. I never heard them have a cross word. We were the all-American happy family. Mom and Dad had no loud arguments, no sordid love affairs, no unwanted or unloved children, no in-law problems. They had enough money to meet our needs. What could all this mean?

"I got sick at my stomach. I could not talk to anyone. After my father moved out, I cried myself to sleep night after night. My mother walked around like a zombie, sad and forlorn, yet convinced she and Dad had made the right move for them.

"Their friends could not understand the arrangement any more than we could. Grandparents, uncles, and aunts called them urging a reconciliation. But nothing seemed to do any good.

"Within a few months they decided to divorce, claiming incompatibility. No other person was involved. My parents simply decided to quit trying to have a marriage. Mother attempted to act pleasant, put the best face possible on the collapse of our home, but she was only partially successful. Everyone who knew her well realized she was breaking up inside.

"When my mother took me to school, I got out of the car,

waited for her to leave, then skipped school. I could not do my work. I did not want to face my friends. All this could not be happening to us—a loving, churchgoing family. God must have really turned against us. But why?

"Four years have passed. We have made new lives for ourselves. My parents have not abandoned us. My father has remarried and I get along all right with his new wife and her children. He gives me no reason at all to doubt his love for me. It still hurts, and here I sit with you guys still trying to figure out what happened to their marriage and how I can avoid such a failure in my own life.

"I do want my parents to be happy, to have good lives for themselves. I really respect their wishes for their own lives. Maybe they did the best they could. My mother has told me that I could not understand, nor could she tell me, everything that happened in their marriage that led up to the collapse. I believe her. Divorce is not easy—ever."

SOME CLUES FOR YOU

We do not intend to stand in judgment on people who feel that they cannot live together anymore. We do urge adults to know that the divorce pain for teenagers is real and that it does help to communicate and include them in the decisions, even the painful ones, involved in the breakup. Adults make the final choices but teenagers have to make their adjustments, either in their own home or in a house with a new step-family.

Young people who experience divorce must work hard to cope with their altered lives. They have to struggle to make right choices so they can ensure as much permanence in their lives as possible. Few families in America escape some brush with divorce, either within the immediate family or in the larger, extended family.

Let us offer some specific clues for you as you struggle to deal with the family divorce that weighs so heavy on your back:

• As impossible as it may sound when divorce occurs, teenagers can live through it. The hurt may choke you sometimes, but Julie, John, Ginger, and countless more youth testify to the fact that you can make it through.

God has not abandoned you. He is present. He knows about and walks with you through your hurt.

• The divorce is *not* your fault. Time and again young people tend to blame themselves for the split between their parents. Sure, your Mom had to nag you about making up your bed or staying out late. Dad complained because you did not cut the grass, accused you of thinking money grows on trees. But those relatively minor irritations did not cause them to divorce. Your parents, for a whole stack of reasons, chose to split up. *You did not do it!*

• In all likelihood you cannot bring your parents back together. No one will fault you for trying. And we can all pray your folks get back together. But you are not a failure when you cannot persuade them to reconcile.

• You need all the help you can get as you face the shock and aftershock of divorce. Please push on through your anger, loneliness, confusion, and fear to seek help for yourself.

• A support group of other teenagers who have experienced family break-up can provide important comfort and guidance. With almost 50 percent of today's marriages ending in divorce, you have plenty of company in your misery. Your minister, high-school counselor or community mental health office can point you toward a good group.

• Make decisions about your own life and stick with them. Only you can finally determine your success or failure in making a life for yourself after a family breakup. John, who was a real, live teenager, made and kept his decisions. Avoid the dead-end road of blaming your parents for your failures. They certainly bear their share of responsibility, but you ultimately make your own life. Do not let their failure shape and break you.

• Deep religious faith does not always prevent divorce. But deep religious faith always helps guide all the involved persons through the divorce. Now is the time for you to dig in deeper into the Bible, into prayer, into church participation—not necessarily in a last-ditch effort to stave off the breakup, but to find the Lord real through the process.

• Besides all these "clues," let us add this important word—keep talking to someone, anyone who will listen. Please do not bottle up your feelings inside.

Julie adds this postscript to her story: "The final breakup of my parent's marriage hurt me even worse because I had no one to talk with. I had played such a game, put on such a brave front that none of my friends knew how badly I hurt. My heartache and frustration became so severe that an English teacher noticed. One day she asked me to remain after class for a minute. She said, 'I have noticed lately that you seem unusually quiet and withdrawn, not at all like yourself. Is something wrong? Do you need to talk with the counselor, a minister—anyone?'

"Her caring for me triggered a flood of tears. We talked

on into the next period. Between her and the counselor I began to deal with my hurt more effectively. My talk with the teacher and other adults did not patch up my parents' marriage, but I began to find ways to deal with my own hurt."

Add your story here if you wish but don't be afraid to admit the hurts you have felt. Find someone you trust to talk with.

TAKE A BREAK·

And the Lord God said, It is not good that the man should be alone; I will make him an help meet for him (Gen. 2:18).

Therefore shall a man leave his father and his mother, and shall cleave unto his wife: and they shall be one flesh (Gen. 2:24).

The Lord is good; he protects his people in times of trouble; he takes care of those who turn to him (Nah. 1:7, GNB).

We know that all things God works for good with those who love him, those whom he has called according to his purpose (Rom. 8:28, GNB).

Do you fear failure because you know that some marriages have failed or because you have been hurt by a marriage failure? Marriage is a noble, godly adventure, designed by God for maximum human happiness. At the right time and place and with the right person, open your-self in love. Teddy Roosevelt believed:

Far better it is to dare mighty things, to win glorious tri-umphs, even though checkered by failure, than to take rank with those poor spirits who neither enjoy much nor suffer much because they live in the gray twilight that knows not victory nor defeat.

Speaking of failure, have you failed this week yourself? I have. Just remember—the miracle of the gospel is forgive-ness and the ability to start over.

10
Just One Drink

ALCOHOL

"Dad?" my voice shook over the phone. "I'm at the police station. They will not release me until you come down and get me."

The kid up the street did not make that call. I did. The kid whose parents were divorced did not make that call. My mom and dad have been married for more than twenty years. The kid who never went to church did not make the call. My family and I attended regularly, yet here I was asking my father to come and get me out of jail.

What I am about to say will sound crazy to many of you living in today's world, but I'll say it anyway and it is the truth: Just one drink landed me in jail. You see, I am a teenage alcoholic. I am not the fun-loving kid portrayed in movies who gets hilariously drunk sometimes. I am not the kid who ties one on at the senior prom then goes on about his business as if nothing ever happened. I tell you the painful truth—I am a seventeen-year-old lush. I cannot handle beer, much less the really hard stuff. It goes right to my head and messes me up but good.

As a growing junior high schooler and early senior high schooler, I had no clue that I would turn into an alcoholic. My parents did not preach against alcohol, though we did sometimes talk about its dangers. My parents drank alcohol a little but they really could not even be called social drinkers. My father would have a can of beer occasionally, and they would order a glass of wine with a meal if they dined out at a nice restaurant. But alcohol was anything but a big deal in our house.

One of my uncles was a drunk, the family black sheep. Uncle Jeff was a good-natured guy sober, but a real loser when he was drunk. Since he drank most of the time, he lost more often than he won. All of us kids laughed at him. We would never be like that!

I remember the first time I was offered a can of beer. The summer before my ninth grade in high school some of the guys picked me up at the house and went riding. My mother knew all the boys so she hardly even noticed as we left. I knew to be home at a decent hour, but I also knew my folks would already be asleep.

We rode around town for a couple of hours, stopped for a hamburger, cruised out by the lake, and began to get bored. After all, how much was there for teenagers to do at night in a town of fifteen-thousand people?

Then the old story repeated a zillion times happened again. One of the guys said, "I know where we can get some beer. Let's pool our money and get a six-pack."

At a little grocery my friend bought the beer—no questions asked. They began to pass the cans around in the car. As a fourteen-year-old boy trying hard to be part of the gang, I found it tough to resist, but I did. I don't know why I said no—maybe my parents' advice, constant warnings by my church leaders, some fear that we would get caught by the police, a vague kind of hesitancy. But, for whatever the reasons, I refused the beer. The guys teased me a bit but they really did not give me a hard time.

They finished the beer, joked and laughed a little bit, and soon, one by one, we headed for home. Nothing happened. We did not have a wreck. The police never even saw us. The boys who did the drinking only seemed to have a better time after they had a few swigs from their cans.

A few nights later the same pattern repeated itself. Same guys. Same routine. But this time I did not refuse the beer. When the can came to me I took a cautious swig. "Ugh, this stuff tastes awful," I sputtered.

"Oh, you'll get used to it" one of my friends promised. And before I had finished the can, he was right. It began to taste better and better.

The one can of beer did not give me much of a buzz, though my body could feel its effects. I guess I felt a little light-headed. At any rate, I felt relieved to find my parents in bed when I got home lest they detect something a little different about me.

I did not immediately begin to want another beer, though I did not forget the sharp taste and the tingle I got from my first can. Looking back I cannot remember exactly when I drank my next can of beer but it happened with the same bunch of friends on much the same kind of night–ride around, get bored, buy a six-pack, and so forth. This time, however, I drank a couple of cans, got a better buzz, but still make it home without incident. My dad called out to me as I came in something like "Have a good time?" And I managed to mumble "yes" as I went into my room.

But this time the slightest bit of yearning crept into my head. I found myself wanting another beer. I remembered that Dad sometimes kept a can in the back side of the refrigerator. One school night, after they were in bed, I slipped into the kitchen and rambled around in the refrigerator and found one can. Before I realized what happened, I popped it open and drank it down real fast. Only the tiniest bell went off in my head. I would have drunk another can if it had been available but I had depleted Dad's "stock" with one slug.

A few days later I heard him ask my mother, "Where is that can of beer I had in the fridg?"

"Oh, honey," she came back, "you probably drank it."

"Maybe so, but I surely don't remember."

Wow! Was I ever relieved! I would have to be more careful next time. Funny thing, even as I thought "next time" I had a strange feeling. Next time? Here I had only had four or five cans of beer in my entire young life and already I was thinking next time. And, you guessed it, before too long I had a next time. But then I added still another wrinkle. Rather than the guys coming by for me, I called up my friend who had a car and suggested we go out riding. Fine. Within an hour or so he and the gang were blowing the horn in front of my house.

As we rode around, I felt myself getting irritated. The bottom-line reason for the ride was not the hamburger or the night view of the lake. I wanted that six-pack. After just a few minutes I heard myself suggesting, casually I hoped, that we stop for the beer. I had money. I would chip in my part. When one of the boys acted like he did not want to stop by the little store where we bought our "booze," I almost yelled.

"All right. All right," the driver of the car shot back. "For crying out loud. Let's go get the man some beer."

While the other guys dawdled over one can, I finished off three and wanted some more but none of us had any more money and we had to get home. I felt nothing from the three cans but I was sure I smelled to high heaven in spite of the mints I had been chewing on. Predictably, Mom and Dad were sacked out so I did not have to pass a breath test.

My drinking grew heavier. Every chance I got, I made arrangements to get some beer. Before too long, I was getting real tipsy. It was fun, but I also began to feel bad about myself. After an evening with the boys, I would slip into the house and fall into bed promising I was not going to drink again, never.

Right. My determination did not last long. By the next day I was getting uptight for something to drink. At first, I was pretty much a weekend drinker. Since I was not old enough to drive, I had to depend on my friends to get me around. I could manage to make it from Saturday night until the next Friday night. But by the middle of that fall I began to look for ways to get out of the house and round up something to drink. And, guess what? I found a new set of friends who would accommodate me. They were week-night drinkers also. They did not worry about schoolwork and had parents who, if they knew what the boys were up to, did not care.

Now, understand, my parents cared a lot for me. But

they both worked and had their own share of problems. The days and weeks slipped by without them really noticing any changes in my life. After a few weeks of dashing out of the house in the middle of the week with my new pals, my mother called me down. "Where are you going?" Who are going with?" I had enough smarts to tell her who the boys were. She did not know them but accepted my explanation that I was studying with them, or that we were just going to ride around for a few minutes. And, after all, Mom, I am getting older and ought to have my privileges expanded.

I had always been a good, average student. I could make top grades in the courses I liked and managed to get by in the rest of them. Believe it or not, with a steadily increasing drinking problem, I kept my grades up. Maybe that says something about my high school. But my report cards showed no slippage.

Looking back on that first year of my drinking, I reached a level of sorts. I could drink enough to feel good, certainly drink up all the extra money I could get my hands on, but my parents never did catch on to what was happening to me. We did some family stuff together on occasion. We kept up our regular church attendance. But they did not know.

My regular school friends began to rib me about being a beer hound, but they were drinking themselves and certainly would never have told their parents for fear of getting themselves in trouble. My younger brother began to catch on. He threatened to tell on me, but I managed to convince him that I was just having an occasional beer. And, besides, Dad has a can of beer every now and then.

Mom and Dad caught me tipsy one night that next summer. I had more than my fill of beer and was, frankly, drunk. In coming into the house I fell and made a big racket. Naturally, Dad jumped out of bed to see what had happened. He knew immediately I had been drinking.

You can imagine the family scene we had that night. Dad yelled. My mother cried. I assured them this was the first and last time such a thing would ever happen to me. I said I had been out with the guys and they, well, forced me into drinking some beer. "One or two cans. That's all. Honest."

They restricted me but tried their best to understand me. I was growing up, making my share of mistakes. Besides, Dad had to confess that, as a teenager, much the same thing had happened to him.

You better believe that I toed the line for several weeks. I managed to survive until they lifted my grounding. As hard as it was, I limited my beer intake. I would stop just short of that one that would push me over the brink. Our house settled into its normal, busy routine.

In the spring, I got my driver's license and found a part-time job. Talk about freedom! I had my own money and pretty well kept my own schedule. I still had an eleven o'clock curfew on weeknights and "be home at a decent hour" on weekends, but my parents did not enforce either limit carefully. And, I say in my own defense, that I made a habit to be home fairly close to the curfew time.

The important difference to me came at the point of freedom and finances to drink. I could handle a lot of beer and had the money to pay for it. What more could a guy ask for?

I know it sounds incredible but my folks did not have a

clue that I was drinking so much. Between their early bed-time and their occasional overnight trips to visit family and friends, I was sailing right along with my little secret.

Occasionally I became concerned about my habit. I knew it was not good for me. I promised myself to lay off. But the very next time I went out, I took on a load.

By the end of the summer I had saved enough to get a car. My Dad and I made a deal. He would help me buy it. I would make enough to pay the insurance and keep it up. We also made an agreement that I had to keep my grades up and stick to the hours we had agreed on. Actually, my folks were quite proud of the way I had worked, saved my money, and now assumed this much responsibility.

The first thing to slide were my grades. Between my job and the increasingly heavier drinking, I could not concentrate. The first report card that fall sounded a warning for my folks and me. They threatened and I promised. The second report card was disastrous—family crisis, session with the high-school counselor.

"Your son is not turning in his homework. He is napping through class. His attitude is rapidly getting terribly careless, indifferent."

I was grounded. I hung up the car keys except for work and school. Result? My grades improved slightly. After appropriate warnings, my parents lifted the restrictions. My grades bombed.

I managed to keep my first DUI ticket from my parents. That stupid cop said I was weaving all over the road. The breath test pronounced me legally drunk. In our state parents did not have to be notified for the first DUI offense. If the youthful offender paid the fine and attended driving school, the ticket did not go on the driving record. The insurance company was notified, but rates were only adjusted once a year, so it would be several months before my Dad found out about my ticket.

I had hardly finished driving school when I got caught again. This time, even in my stupor, I knew I was in big trouble. My folks would find out. Like an idiot I tried to resist arrest. I got rowdy with the officer. He took me into the station. And, then came the phone call.

You can imagine how absolutely staggered my parents were. The subject of my drinking had not been raised since that time many months before when my dad had caught me drunk.

I first tried to lie my way out. But over the next weeks my drinking problem came out. Once alerted, my folks put any television private eye to shame. From friends, my brother, from anxious store clerks where I bought my beer, they got the whole sorry story.

Overnight our house changed. My parents kept up with every move my brother and I made. They got me in a "program." My drinking came to a screeching halt. Slowly, life began to return to its old patterns. My parents began to breathe easy again. Restrictions eased, then all but vanished.

Then came the wreck. Fortunately I was not driving. The officer called my parents to come get me at the station. They were relieved that no one got hurt. But their relief vanished like smoke when the officer told them how much booze they had found in the wrecked car. The wily policeman also, off the record, told my folks that all of us in the car were stinking drunk. We were lucky no one was injured or that we had not hurt someone else.

The wreck and its revelations convinced my parents that I had a severe drinking problem. I screamed that I did not, that I only drank a little, that I could quit any time I wanted to. Leave me alone, I said. But I was in real trouble. I guess the shock of the wreck, the embarrassment of the officer's story, and my parent's angry dismay pushed me over the brink. I sneaked out of the house at night to get something to drink. I would bribe friends to slip me a can while I worked. Of course, my dad did not keep any alcohol at home. In short, I nearly drove everyone absolutely bananas, especially myself.

My folks became unofficial experts in dealing with a teenage alcoholic. I hate to think how much money they spent or how many hours they agonized over my problem with me yelling and acting like a fool most of the time. I would not admit that I had a problem. I still maintained that I could handle it all myself.

Some kids have to go through an overwhelming crisis before they begin to turn around, if they ever begin at all. My story is somewhat different. We had along series of mini-crises that had the net effect of wearing me down. I bounced from one program to another with not much noticeable effect. I suppose the most help came when I understood that my basic problem was the total incapacity of my body to manage alcohol. The whole cluster of teenage pressures had combined to get alcohol on my back—peer pressure, craving for new adventure, slightly distracted parents, the lack of substantial alcohol education from church and school. But I came to realize I was an alcoholic and always would be. I would never be able to drink alcohol and stay on top.

The variations on this story are just about infinite. You could tell your own personal experience about teenage drinking and alcoholism. The real danger to you as a teenager is to say to yourself, "Well, that could never happen to me." Stop kidding yourself. You know it could happen to you. What right do you have to exempt yourself from the rest of teenage humanity!

Without any effort at recall we could spiel off half a dozen horror stories involving teenage drinking and alcoholism. Automobile accidents resulting in disfigurement and permanent handicap. Young lives snuffed out in grinding auto collisions. Promising athletic and academic careers smashed. Terrible pain and suffering to family and friends. All immediately traceable to alcohol.

TAKE A BREAK

I would have you learn this great fact: that a life of doing right is the wisest life there is. If you live that kind of life you'll not limp or stumble as you run. Carry out my instructions; don't forget them, for they will lead you to real living (Prov. 4:11-13).

The Lord is faithful, and he will strengthen you and keep you from the Evil One (2 Thess. 3:3, GNB).

Submit yourselves to God. Resist the Devil, and he will run away from you. Come near to God, and he will come near to you. Humble yourselves before the Lord, and he will lift you up (Jas. 4:7-8, 10, GNB).

1. Name a mistake that you have made; a time that you think that you did wrong. Think about the circumstances that surrounded that decision.

2. Can you accept the forgiveness of God? Can you forgive yourself. Remember that Peter was given a second chance when he denied that he knew Christ.

3. Make an imaginary game plan to help you avoid tough situations where a decision will have to be made.

"Lead us not into temptation . . ." Stop right now and pray the Lord's Prayer. Accept the strength that comes from His Spirit.

List three temptations you need the Lord's help with:

1.

2.

3.

11
The Ultimate Anger

SUICIDE

These are the best years of my life? Wrong! Or, at least, I hope not. This year has been a real bummer for me. Three of my friends tried to commit suicide. One of my friends succeeded. Maybe I should also.

What causes a person, especially a teenager, with all of life beckoning, to want to end life, or in fact end his or her life?

Perhaps these stories can give some clues.

I CUT MY WRISTS

It was not something I did on the spur of the moment. For a long, long time, I had imagined ways to kill myself. The emotion to die would sweep over me like a wave. In fact, if anything happened to upset me—a fight with my brother, an argument with my parents, anything—the first thought that jumped into my mind was, I should just kill myself. My next thought would be, "Not really" then, "They will be sorry." I always fantasized how *they* would feel to see me dead. Then maybe they would be truly sorry they did not treat me right or let me have what I wanted.

This feeling, this unpredictable urge, plagued me all the time. I usually made good grades in school, but if I did not get a good grade, if I did not have my homework, or if I got in trouble with one of my teachers, my reaction was invariably the same. "I should kill myself, then they can't make me do any work or embarrass me anymore."

Rejection made me feel the worst of all. You can imagine how I felt when my boyfriend decided we should break up. He was wrong if he thought everything would be all right by saying we could still be friends, that we both needed some space and time. He did not care that I really loved him, that I did not want to break up. He was so cold! The old feelings about killing myself flared up. I would kill myself, then he would miss me and be really sorry for what he did.

Perhaps it was a combination of all the experiences and problems I had run into that pushed me over the brink. Maybe I had just said "suicide" to myself so long. Anyway, one day after school it happened. I had had a terrible day. My best girl friend and I fought all day long. I was still hurting from the breakup with my boyfriend. I felt like I had lost all my best friends.

On the way home I decided I had no reason to live any longer. I was crossed up with everyone and everyone was treating me bad. None of them cared whether I lived or died. They would be relieved for me to get out of the way. I felt low, really low.

An easy out, that's what I wanted. I had thought about

the method many times but the quickest, easiest way seemed to be to cut my wrists.

I went home and walked into the kitchen. I never even stopped to think. I took out a sharp butcher knife, slashed away at my wrists and fell to the floor. I do not remember anything else until the ambulance came and roared off to the hospital with me.

People have asked what I thought about as I lay on the floor before passing out. I did not think anything at all. As far as I was concerned, life for me was over. On the way to the hospital, I came to enough to realize I was not dead. But even that realization made no difference to me, either way.

I did not die. Maybe I did not really want to die. At the time, I had no hesitation about my own death. It seemed the best course for me. The doctors and my parents have spent a great deal of time with me since then trying to help me get a grip on my life. We have talked for hours and hours about the reasons why I attempted suicide and how to avoid another such episode.

Today I am glad it did not work. My parents and I have learned a great deal about our individual lives and our family life. I have begun to find other ways to think, other things to do when life deals me a bad blow. Thanks to all the conversation, especially with some of the professional people who have worked with me, I see more clearly the reasons people do not want to live. Disappointments and hurts do not throw me like they used to. Most of all, I am learning that I am an important person in my own right with good hopes and dreams. I have come to understand that my life has meaning and that God has a purpose for my life.

I hate to think that I wanted to get even with people. Maybe I did. But I get really scared when I think how close I came to losing my own life. It did not dawn on me how "forever" that decision could have been. I am on the road to having a good life. It's too bad I almost ended it before I found out how much life has to offer.

MY BROTHER SUCCEEDED

My brother committed suicide. Though it happened several years ago, I still live that scene over and over again.

John and I had a close relationship, more than many brothers and sisters do. Maybe we felt close because of our ages. We were only eighteen months apart. When we were little, mother even dressed us in matching boy-girl outfits. Some people even thought we were twins. The main reason for our closeness, however, was that we faced a common problem—a hopelessly alcoholic father. Dad did not abuse us physically but he battered us emotionally, making home one long ordeal.

We both excelled at school. We made very good grades, became school leaders and athletes, had many friends, and made a happy life for ourselves away from home. We overcame the hardships of home and did well in school because we had each other to draw from. In every way we supported and encouraged one another. Big Brother John paved the way for little sister. We helped each other laugh rather than cry at tough situations. He drove me everywhere before I got my license. John would pick up my friends and me and take us around rather than have them come to our house and run the risk of having a bad scene with my father.

As John and I got older, my father seemed to get worse. Unless you have lived with an alcoholic, you cannot imagine what we went through. My mother gradually became remote from Dad and from us. She worked, but spent much of her time doing her own thing—tennis with friends, getting her hair done, shopping. She loved us, we knew that. Probably in self-defense she just drifted away from the family. But no matter what happened, John and I made it through together. He was light in my darkness.

Throughout high school John did great. He had high moral standards and worked hard at everything he did.

During the fall of his senior year, John's football coach suggested that a college football scholarship might be out there somewhere. The coach's confidence made John work that much harder. I just knew he would make it.

One afternoon, soon after the season ended, I looked up and there came John strolling down the hall toward me. "Sis," he said, with a frown on his face, "I've got to talk with you. It's serious."

My heart stopped for a moment.

Then he burst into a smile and yelled, "I got the scholarship! They want me to play for them! They picked only me from this entire area!"

I could not have been more pleased. But I also had some pangs of regret when I realized he would be away at school next year. Could I make it by myself?

Maybe all the success finally got to John or maybe life had simply caught up with my brother. Whatever happened, the results proved tragic. After years of right choices, he began making bad choices. During the spring of the year, after the sports season ended and John had secured the coveted scholarship, he decided to enjoy himself, become part of the group—he decided to drink. Everyone around him enjoyed alcohol in moderation, why not John, he reasoned. I do not know exactly what happened, but gradually he and I spent less and less time together. He was finishing his senior year and I was caught up in the end of school myself. I did not particularly notice the changes in him and in our relationship.

He and I had a great time when he graduated. In spite of my father's condition, John, Mother, and I celebrated his achievement. He and some of his friends took a senior trip to the beach but came back home on schedule.

As the summer went by he spent more time with friends and less around the house. He stayed out late more often. But, after all, he had graduated from high school. I missed him but had a job that kept me busy. Looking back, I realize something was not quite right with him, but I attributed the difference to his graduation and thinking about college.

One day, to my surprise and delight he said, "Keep Thursday night open. I want us to go out before I leave." He seemed unusually serious, but I concluded he was getting college jitters.

We had a night like a hundred others. We picked up some friends, got something to eat, talked, and laughed. I enjoyed every minute of the evening. We talked about college, about high school, about our relationship, about Mother and Dad. When we got back home, John gave me a brotherly talk about watching out for certain groups the next year in school. He warned me about some teachers and what courses to take and not to take. As we started to bed, he gave me a big hug and told me goodnight.

I had no more conversations with my brother.

The next day I came home from work to find the house filled with neighbors and friends. We all usually arrived home from work around 6 o'clock. The routine was that Mom came in first, then me, then John, and finally Dad, that is if he did not stop too long at his favorite bar. Anyway, when I came home on this particular day, I was surprised to see John's car in the driveway, not to mention all the other people. I knew something terrible had happened. I hurried inside to see my mother collapsed in tears with a look of horror on her face.

Then they told me what had happened.

John had come home early, gone into my room, written me a long letter that he put on my dresser, stretched out on my bed, took a gun, and shot himself!

I still do not believe it happened—even as I tell it.

Mother came home, saw his car in the driveway, called for him, looked for him through the house and found him in my room. The scene, as she described it, remains etched in my brain. I was in shock and, to some extent, I still am.

His letter to me simply stated that he knew I loved him and would be the only person to truly understand why he took his life. He wanted me to know that he loved me very much and did not intend to hurt me, but he felt he had to do this or he would inflict pain on too many other people. He begged me to forgive him. He felt that to live would be to perpetuate an illness from which we had suffered so deeply already.

He went on to tell me that he had begun to drink heavily that spring. He could not quit drinking when he tried. Then he concluded he was an incurable alcoholic like our father. He just knew he would wind up like Dad and could not stand that thought. This was the best way to solve the problem for all concerned. "I hope you will understand. Love, John"

No! No! No! John, I do not understand. I do not understand why you did not talk with me or with someone. I do not understand why you wouldn't try to get some help. We had shared so much. Why stop at a time like this! I do not understand how you could walk away from college, scholarship, football, friends—all your dreams.

I do not understand how you could come to my room, die on my bed, and expect me to understand. I do not. I will never understand. I will always miss you. I will always feel deep, deep sadness that you did this. Maybe this was your way of expressing ultimate anger at Dad for his drinking, for passing it on to you. Maybe you were angry at Mom for living her own life with so little regard for our problems. Or, maybe, you were just tired. I do not know, but you can be sure I do not understand. I believe your death was a horrible, horrible waste. I will spend much of my life trying to understand so I can help others avoid this kind of final tragedy.

SUICIDE

Suicide defies explanation. Many psychologists, psychiatrists, and other professionals have tried for years to understand this ultimate experience. These experts have studied, analyzed, probed the lives and reactions of suicidal patients and clients. The conclusions have come out as diverse as the analyzers and patients involved. Some suicides (or attempts) can be explained by depression, despair, frustration, illness, substance abuse, rage, meaninglessness of life, and so on. None of the answers satisfy all the situations. None of the suppositions truly satisfy the overriding concerns that life is over for that individual. Suicide rings down the curtain *forever*.

Some Remembers:

• Remember, life is a gift. No matter how frightened or frustrated you become, another day will dawn. As Robert Schuller says: "Tough times don't last; tough people do."

• Remember, people are out "there" who want to help you and can help you. If you begin to feel depressed, suicidal, *run, do not walk* to some of those people—your counselor, your minister, your friend, your parents.

• Remember, you have time on your side. When the urge comes to take those pills, cut your wrists, drive your car into the bridge abutment, or whatever, stop that thought! Call your friend, neighbor, parent. You do not even have to talk about your feelings. Just talk with another living human being. Go somewhere—the shopping center, zoo, church, library, movie—anywhere you can find people.

Your judgment can be impaired by chemicals or by an emotion. Give yourself *time* to look clearly at your situation. Psychiatrists say the urge to commit suicide does not last long. If you can give yourself some time, interrupt your pattern of thinking, you will buy yourself time, time to look realistically at your life.

• Remember, suicide lasts *forever!* Suicide does far more

than provide a moment of revenge, to hear people say, "I am sorry." *You* are the victim. Others will grieve and suffer, but you pay the price for the longest amount of time—forever. You lose—forever.

• Remember, God loves you and wants to walk with you in this life. He can give you direction, peace, and comfort in the middle of your problems. God will give you strength to manage even the most difficult of situations. Ask Him to lead you to that person to help unravel those troubling thoughts that plague you. All you have to do is ask—God and anyone of a dozen people around you.

TAKE A BREAK

Even those who are admired and extolled have "holes" that God dug them out of.

> With Moses it was murder.
> With Elijah it was deep depression.
> With Peter it was public denial.
> With Samson it was recurring lust.
> With Thomas it was cynical doubt.
> With Jacob it was deception.
> With Rahab it was prostitution.
> With Jephthah it was illegitimate birth.

Look to the rock from which you were hewn, and to the quarry [hole] from which you were digged (Isa. 51:1, RSV).

The Lord is good, a strong hold in the day of trouble; and he knows them that trust in him (Nah. 1:7).

In everything you do, put God first, and he will direct you and crown your efforts with success (Prov. 3:6, TLB).

1. Console someone today who is having a time in a "hole" in their lives.

2. Look at your own past and be grateful for coming through those "low-tide" days.

3. Take a pencil and paper and list the names of some people you can call when you feel especially low.

12
The Bottom Line

FAITH

The ashen-faced teenager sank down in the chair in my office. With tears darting to her eyes and wringing her hands, she choked out the words I had heard countless times: "My life is totally hopeless and meaningless. I don't have anything to live for. I wish I could die!"

My young friend had been involved in an angry, hysterical family fight that exploded into the death of her brother. The police, the courts and, worst of all, her family, held her directly responsible for the young man's death. The shooting had occurred more than six months prior to my encounter with her. Immediately after the death, she dropped out of high school, shrinking away into a cocoon of grief and guilt with nothing from her family but recrimination. The juvenile authorities finally insisted she either get back in school or go to a state reformatory. Accepting the advice of former teachers and counselors, her father moved her into a new school where few, if any, students would know of the death episode. So, here she sat begging, more with her eyes than her words, for help and security as she ventured back into school.

After only a few minutes with the young lady, I knew she would have a tough time succeeding in high school. At that get-acquainted session, she told me of the persistent nightmares that plagued her restless sleep. Examining her previous high-school records I found out she had never done well in school, primarily because of the tumultuous, violent home situation in which she had grown up.

Days went by. Nearly every morning she turned up in my office, always in shambles. We talked about the death and her involvement. I must have heard the story a half-dozen times as she repeated it again and again to me. In spite of her muddled thinking, our relationship grew stronger. Conversation flowed easily between us.

Though her classmates knew nothing about her past, the guilt she felt walled her away from them. Some of the students tried to make friends with her, but she rebuffed them. "Forget it," the other students said by word and deed, thus deepening her sense of isolation and frustration.

In spite of the combined efforts of psychologists, high-school counselors, administrators and teachers, her schoolwork continued to suffer. She simply could not concentrate, so shattered was she by the death and the years of disrupted home life that led up to that crashing moment.

One particular day, when life proved especially difficult, she flung herself into my office. She threatened to take her own life since nothing seemed to matter. In response, I moved into territory we had not explored before. "Have you been to church with Joan yet?"

Joan, a mutual friend, had invited her often.

With a fierce bitterness in her voice, the tormented student shot back, "If you are asking me if I am a Christian, the answer is *no!* And I never will be. I am not interested, period! I am not sure I even believe in God. I may believe in God. I am still living for some reason. But I certainly am not going to be a Christian and I will not start attending church."

I reached out to her and said, "That's too bad. Faith is your only hope. As you say, 'It is the bottom line.'"

What is faith? Why is faith the bottom line?

In a thousand different ways, in a thousand varying life situations, teenagers ask these faith questions.

TELL ME ABOUT GOD

In one of my twelfth-grade English classes, I had a young man who had everything money could buy. He also had trophies from athletic achievements and honors for academic excellence. Many in the class envied him because he seemed to have been born with a silver spoon in his mouth.

One day after school he came to my desk and said, "I need to talk with you."

Teachers always have more going on than they can manage and I was no exception. What's more, students regularly hovered around my desk saying they needed to talk with me. Rather nonchalantly, I have to admit, though with genuine interest, I said "Sure. Talk away," and I went on about my business of grading papers as he began to talk.

He began to talk while I listened and graded. But in a moment, the young student quietly but emphatically pleaded between his teeth, "Would you please stop what you are doing and pay attention to me! I want you to tell me about God."

He got my attention.

I did exactly what he asked. I put aside my work and drove with him to the small-town drugstore and hung to the words of the bright, silver-spooned student. For the rest of the period, and on into the next one, we talked. He asked me all the faith questions, probing my every thought, picking my brain about my own ideas of faith, religion, and the way to understand himself before God.

Knowing that Bob was pastor of one of the local churches, he felt free to ask, "Why are you a Christian?"

I looked back over my own experience. I explained I could not imagine life without faith in Jesus Christ. I told him of my childhood faith and deepening faith as I grew older. We talked about our creation in the image of God and the innate yearning we have to know God in a personal way.

Through his studies, this bright, gifted young man had come to sense that life held more than met the eye. He sensed a power in the universe, perhaps even a Person in the universe whom he wanted to know. In short, he wanted faith. He wanted to satisfy a very deep part of his life, a part of his own being that flowed from God.

Deciding he needed to pursue his questions, I suggested he talk with Bob who explained the simplicity of believing in God, of relying on His love, and of returning that love through daily living.

In time, the young man got excited and opened himself to a pilgrimage of faith that has endured until this day. He has grown up, completed college, entered a profession, and taken on family responsibilities, but his pilgrimage is not over. That day he started at the bottom-line faith in God.

Quickly realizing the necessity for growth, he became active in a church, turned on to worship, and learned about the different doctrines. He chose to be baptized in a Protestant church and shared his newfound faith with family and friends. He began serious study of the Bible to learn more fully what his faith is all about. He found the hope and adventure that the people across the ages have found. He decided the bottom line to living is faith in God; not a blind, Pollyanna idea that everything in life is rosy, but a strong confidence in the reality of a power beyond ourselves.

LET'S TALK ABOUT FAITH—FOR YOU

Life for you, teenager, is often unsure. No matter where you live or what wonderful or horrible people you live with, you find yourself feeling fearfully alone sometimes. Every person, no matter how outgoing or popular, no matter how quiet and withdrawn, feels cut off from others at one time or another. When those feelings come, don't panic. You may be in the middle of a crowd and have a wave of loneliness sweep over you. Loneliness is a normal reaction to being human. Successful living lies in managing any or all of the human emotions, loneliness included. The young person who is able to feel alone, who is able to cope with that feeling with himself or herself, is more likely able to cope with the problems and experiences of life, good or bad. This coping power comes from faith in God through Jesus Christ. Faith rooted in Scripture assures us we are never truly alone. This measure of faith assures us we are

loved regardless of the circumstances in which we find ourselves. It also assures us that we can return that love to God
and to others.

Faith in God brings the quiet confidence that He made us
and likes what He made. You may be critical of yourself—
your body, your personality, your abilities. We all struggle
with self-criticisms. But faith in God comes to impress us
with His stamp of approval. God is proud of you. He is ever-
lastingly glad He made you.

The life of bottom-line faith has many benefits.

As a starter, the life of faith *promises* you a *purpose* for
life. God wants you to do something special with your life.
The birth of faith in your life is not just a one-shot deal. It
is, as the young man discovered, a lifetime of exploring, of
new openings of yourself, your gifts, your talents, your cre-
ativity.

God is the Enabler, the Guide as you discover your purpose through the use of your abilities. I have always de-
lighted to remember that not only did God give us our
abilities, He helps us find and develop them. He plants our
talents within us, then sets about to help us discover what
He has put there.

Until my middle-thirties, public speaking terrified me. I
could talk all day long to classes and small groups, but
standing before a crowd making a speech made me want to
run away. Then I was elected executive director of the
Georgia National Honor Society, a position that required
public addresses to educators, civic clubs, and large bodies
of students. I wanted the position, intended to do a good
job with the task, and simply decided I would do public
speaking in spite of my pounding heart and dry mouth. In

just a short time I grew to enjoy the opportunity to make speeches. I still have anxieties, but the anxieties nearly always give way to the satisfaction of knowing my ideas are being considered by inquiring people. The ability to speak lay inside my personality, placed there by God. Rising to opportunity and adventure freed my God-given gifts.

The promise of purpose also helps us deal with the failures that are sure to come. If you do not "knock 'em dead" in one venture, you have the freedom to turn to go another way. This promise of purpose assures us there are no locks and keys on your future, only a process of opened and closed doors. You are free to try and fail. The amazing discovery for me is that nearly always in a failure. I discover the stuff, the ingredients of success along a new path.

For instance, a student friend of Bob's was pastor of a small church near our college town. He asked Bob to try out for a position as minister of music in his church. Bob had only limited experience in church music but, wanting to be of service and also in need of a job, he accepted the friend's offer. After only a few hours into the interview weekend, Bob and the music committee realized this was *not* a relationship made in heaven. The committee kindly, but emphatically, informed Bob he was not the one for their church. Discouragement. Hurt feelings. But not for long. Reading the want ads in the college newspaper, Bob learned that a large florist who sold corsages for football games needed a campus salesman. No matter that Bob knew nothing about flowers. He took the job, made the money he needed, established hundreds of new friendships, and discovered some brand-new gifts that had not surfaced before. Out of one failure came success from a completely unexpected quarter.

Purpose, then *perception*. Faith gives you fresh perception, a new outlook. Once you let bottom-line faith get inside of you, people, including yourself, "look" different. Suddenly people are not just masses, they become people. You see people who have needs, problems, and hang-ups, but who also have worth and potential.

This new perception adds new meaning, new maturity to our lives. Don't get me wrong. You will not automatically *mature*. Maturing, new depth, and fresh perceptions come over time. Even Jesus had to grow in stature and in human relationships. People grow in stages and processes. For instance, it is natural for teenagers to giggle and snicker one minute and share their deepest thoughts and faith with a friend the next. But there is a depth difference if you have allowed bottom-line faith into your life.

Underneath it all, as you grow and mature, you have the assurance that God is in control of your life. This assurance allows us to celebrate living. If you allow your faith to be the adventure that God wants it to be, you will truly celebrate living. And make no mistake, we all have a deep need to celebrate life, to find ways to express the job of being alive.

Finding bottom-line faith enables us to deal with death. Teenagers do not like to think about death, but it grabs youth like it does other people.

Our community was rocked to its bones by the death of four teenagers who lost their young lives in a grinding automobile wreck. Three of them died instantly and one died the next day without ever regaining consciousness. The students, all seniors, attended the same high school. They were the popular kids: football players, drill team members, student council members. What blinding tragedy for the hundreds of friends and the families to endure! What could the mourning students say to each other as they moved from homes, to funeral chapels, to churches? How could they look at those caskets, sing the hymns, go through the liturgies? How could they escape a similar fate? What could sixteen-year-olds say to parents of their friends?

They could *all* endure this tragedy with tears, questions, and frustrations. But for those who had faith in the living Lord they could go through with hope; a hope that does not end with death. It was a sign of hope as teenagers walked to the caskets and knelt to make a sign of the cross. It was a sign of hope as teenagers took a flower and placed it on the casket or the newly-made grave. It was a sign of hope as teenagers hugged each other and remembered. It was a sign of hope as teenagers gathered days later to talk about death and what it all meant. It was a sign of hope when they could say, "Someday we will see them again." Faith is the bottom line to living and dying.